dolci

francine segan

photographs by ellen silverman

dolci
italy's sweets

Stewart, Tabori & Chang, New York

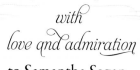

with
love and admiration
to Samantha Segan,
my sweet and talented daughter

Published in 2011 by Stewart, Tabori & Chang
An imprint of ABRAMS

Text copyright © Francine Segan
All photographs copyright © 2011 by Ellen Silverman, except:
pages 3, 143: Shutterstock; page 15: Perugina chocolates; pages 19, 100, 128: Corsini Biscotti; pages 27, 32: Falanga-Sabra; page 63: Ferrero; page 69: De Bondt
Chocolate; page 73: Bauli; page 104: Amarelli licorice; pages 107, 190–191: Consorzio dell'Asti D.O.C.G.; pages 139, 165: Franca Artuso; page 147: Pinella Orgiana;
pages 172, 175: AIDEPI; page 187: Emilia Romagna Region Tourist Board

Library of Congress Cataloging-in-Publication Data

Segan, Francine.
    Dolci : Italy's sweets / Francine Segan.
        p. cm.
    Includes bibliographical references and index.
    ISBN 978-1-58479-898-9 (alk. paper)
    1. Desserts—Italy. 2. Pastry—Italy. 3. Cooking, Italian. 4. Cookbooks. I. Title.
    TX773.S3546 2010
    641.8'60946—dc22
                                    2010048546

Project Editor: Marisa Bulzone
Art Director: Michelle Ishay-Cohen
Designer: Laura Klynstra
Production Manager: Anet Sirna-Bruder

The text of this book was composed in Tychno & Lisboa.

Printed and bound in China
10 9 8 7 6 5 4 3 2 1

Stewart, Tabori & Chang books are available at special discounts when purchased in quantity for premiums and promotions as well as fundraising or educational use.
Special editions can also be created to specification. For details, contact specialsales@abramsbooks.com or the address below.

ABRAMS
THE ART OF BOOKS SINCE 1949
115 West 18th Street
New York, NY 10011
www.abramsbooks.com

introduction

None of the recipes in this book are actually mine. That might sound odd coming from a cookbook author, but it's true. It takes a village to raise a child? Well, you might say it took an entire country to write this cookbook.

I gathered the recipes from all corners of Italy, from hundreds of generous, enthusiastic Italians eager to share their country's culinary traditions. They opened their homes, kitchens, pantry cabinets, recipe files, and hearts to me. The recipes come from all of them, and the result represents their work as well as mine. Each person spent many hours with me, either in Italy, or on the phone, via e-mail, or on Skype. They helped me comb through details and nuances until finally I was able to re-create reliably what I had so enjoyed in Italy.

The recipes come from:

- Homemakers and nonprofessional cooks—from hip young food bloggers to grandmas in villages so remote they had no Internet connection.
- Important Italian pastry manufacturers, including Bauli, Corsini, and Falanga, who not only provided recipes, but also hosted factory visits and arranged meetings with local historians and chefs.
- Restaurant chefs, including an octogenarian so revered for his contributions to Italian cuisine that he received the title Cavaliere, the equivalent of knighthood.
- Pastry chefs ranging from the proprietors of simple six-seat cafés to famous TV personalities.
- Cooking school instructors, including Sorelle Simile—the Simile sisters—Italy's famed twins with the apt last name that means "similar."
- Bake shop and pastry store owners.

- Italian foodie websites, many of which, like the delightful *Un Tocco di Zenzero*, posted bulletins asking readers to help me.
- Italian cookbooks made available to me by private collectors, monasteries, and the library at Academia Barilla in Parma.
- Italian tourism boards and industry consortia specializing in everything from Asti Spumante DOCG sparkling wine to DOP radicchio.
- Italian food writers and journalists who, as if by magic, could always put me in touch with a friend who had a cousin who knew someone who would teach me that special recipe I'd been trying to track down for weeks.

notes on the recipes

the ingredients

Candied fruit

Candied fruit peel or candied fruit is found in many traditional Italian desserts, adding moisture, concentrated bursts of flavor, and a lovely aroma. Fine Italian candied fruits and peels are artisan products made by a long, labor-intensive process.

If, for whatever reason, you don't like candied fruit, then by all means leave it out of any recipe—or substitute dried apricots, golden raisins, or other dried fruit instead.

Flour

Most Italian desserts are made with 00 flour.

Italy and the United States categorize flour differently. In the United States, flour is defined by the amount of protein it contains. In Italy, flour is defined by how finely it is ground: ranging from 2—which is coarsely ground—to 1, then 0, and finally the very fine 00 that is used for bread, pizza, and desserts.

Italian 00 is like our cake or pastry flour in texture, but has a higher protein content, so it bakes more like our all-purpose flour.

Technically, the recipes in this book will "work" if you substitute all-purpose flour for the 00 flour; however, if you want to obtain both the texture and rise of Italian 00 flour, substitute a 1:1 ratio mix of all-purpose flour and cake flour.

Gelatin

In the United States, gelatin is most commonly found in powder form and sold in envelopes (1 envelope is about ¼ ounces or 7 grams, which is roughly 2¼ teaspoons). In Italy it is most commonly found in sheets of various sizes and weights.

If you are using sheet gelatin instead of powdered, follow the package directions for use and conversions. As you'll note, sheet gelatin must be softened in cold water before use. In general, use the same gram weight of standard supermarket-brand sheet gelatin as powdered gelatin (1 envelope gelatin powder equals about 7 to 8 grams of sheet gelatin).

Leavening

If you like, use an Italian leavening for sweets that is called *lievito per dolci* in place of double-acting baking powder. Several companies make it, most notably Paneangeli and Bertolini. It often comes with a pinch of vanilla, so you can use less in the recipe. One envelope is sufficient for one average cake.

Mosto cotto

Mosto cotto is a dense, sweet, cooked must syrup made from wine grapes. It has been a popular sweetener, especially in southern Italy, since ancient Greek times. In Abruzzo, Calabria, Puglia, Sicily, and other parts of southern Italy it is used in various cookie recipes and to sweeten *cuccia*, a cooked wheatberry dessert eaten on December 13 to celebrate Santa Lucia Day.

Nuts

Italy has exceptionally delicious nuts, and many Italian sweets, such as *torrone, panforte*, marzipan, and *gianduia*, feature nuts. There are hundreds of nut-based desserts in Italy and I've included dozens in this book including Almond Biscotti (page 18), Honey-Walnut Chocolate Glazed Pie (page 92), and Almond Granita (page 106).

Each region of Italy has its own specialty nuts and several nuts have been given special IGP designation (protected geographic status). The same nut—hazelnuts, for example—are so different that two types, each of which has been awarded IGP status: the hazelnuts of Piedmont (*tonde gentile delle Langhe*) as well as the hazelnuts of Campania (*nocciola di Giffoni* or *tonda di Giffoni*).

Some tips when baking with nuts:

* Be sure to buy only the best-quality nuts, and to check the expiration date, as nuts go stale quickly. Taste them before use to double-check that they are still fresh. Store nuts in the freezer or refrigerator in an air-tight container.
* For best results, toast nuts before using to release all their flavor and aroma. It's best done in the oven for a more uniformly toasted, drier, and more flavorful nut. Usually 10 minutes at 350°F (180°C), until golden and fragrant, does the trick.
* Many recipes call for nut flours, like hazelnut or almond flour. Nut flours can be found in gourmet shops or purchased online. Or you can make your own. Toast the nuts whole in the oven, let cool to room temperature, then finely grind in a small food processor or coffee grinder. Just take care not to over-grind or you'll begin to create nut butter.

Raw Eggs

Many traditional Italian desserts like Traditional Tiramisù (page 131) and "Instant" Chocolate Cake (page 75) call for raw eggs. Raw egg whites add volume and raw yolks add richness and moisture.

There are several options if you'd prefer not to use raw eggs:

* Pasteurized shell eggs such as Safest Choice brand are my favorite choice for a totally safe raw egg product. They have been specially pasteurized while still in the shell to destroy salmonella bacteria.
* Powdered egg whites work well as a substitute for raw egg whites. Reconstitute the egg-white powder and whip just as you would fresh uncooked egg whites.
* Cook the eggs, yolks, or whites with sugar and a bit of water over a pot of simmering water until they reach a temperature of 160°F (71°C).
* You can substitute whipped cream for egg whites.

Vanilla bean

In Italy, many home cooks grate a vanilla pod on a Microplane and use the resulting specs instead of pure vanilla extract. I find it an easier technique than scraping the inside seeds, plus it uses the entire bean.

For any of the recipes here, you may substitute grated vanilla pod for vanilla extract. Depending on the quality of the vanilla pod you are using, 1 tablespoon extract equals about ½ grated pod.

General Baking Tips

To roll out dough:

I learned a fabulous tip in Italy.

When rolling out dough, instead of putting flour on a work surface to keep the dough from sticking, spread out clean white cotton canvas cloth instead. It works miracles.

The dough doesn't stick or dry out from absorbing the extra flour. Plus—and this is a big deal for me—clean-up is much easier. No little stuck-on bits of flour all over the place. Just toss the cloth in the washing machine when you're done and enjoy your dessert! It's inexpensive and available at any fabric store. Try it when making the Sweet Chickpea Baked Ravioli (page 138) or *Carteddate* (page 164).

Temperature of Ingredients

All refrigerated ingredients, like eggs, milk, and butter should be used at room temperature.

Measurements

Italians are not generally the type of cooks that measure ingredients very precisely—except that they *always* weigh flour and key ingredients when baking. For best results, weigh all key ingredients.

For non-key ingredients, I have used the highly imprecise "handful" where the precise, exact measure is not critical and can be adjusted to the cook's taste.

For those of you who prefer precision here's a conversion chart:

ONE SMALL HANDFUL = ¼ TO ⅓ CUP
HANDFUL = ½ CUP
LARGE HANDFUL = ¾ TO 1 CUP

CHAPTER ONE

cookies and
bite-sized sweets

BISCOTTI E PASTICCINI

PREVIOUS SPREAD FROM LEFT: VENICE'S CORNMEAL COOKIES (PAGE 24),
RED WINE RINGS (PAGE 26), AND ABSURDLY ADDICTIVE HONEY COOKIES (PAGE 13)

absurdly addictive honey cookies

Mustazzoli

MAKES ABOUT 2 DOZEN

REGION: Sicily

Made with just two ingredients—honey and flour—*mustazzoli* epitomize the fundamental Italian culinary rule that less is more! Honey is the star here, so be sure to pick a dark, dense one with a rich, deep flavor. The famed Antica Dolceria Bonajuto in Modica, where I learned this recipe, uses local Sicilian carob honey, which is medium-dark in color with a wine-like richness and aroma. Other good choices include buckwheat or prickly pear–cactus honey.

The Sicilians say these cookies "keep you company," meaning that they are so chewy, it takes ages to eat one. They're even given to toddlers as a sort of teething ring.

Preheat the oven to 400°F (200°C). Line a baking sheet with parchment paper.

Put the honey into a bowl, and slowly add in the flour, mixing with your fingers until a dough forms. It will be dense and sticky. Depending on the amount of moisture in the honey you are using, you may need to add more flour.

Coat your hands with flour. Gently, using your palms, roll the dough right on the baking sheet into a log about 13 inches (33 centimeters) long and 1 inch (2.5 centimeters) thick. If the dough comes apart, just roll it into a ball and reconnect the parts; working from the center, slowly roll it out into a log shape. The heat of your hands helps to warm the honey, which acts like glue for the flour.

Cut the log, on an angle, into 1¼-inch (3-centimeter) sections. Don't try to completely separate the sections at this point—the dough is too sticky. Or, if you prefer, you can separate the sections and form them into little swirled S-shapes, as shown in the photo on page 10.

Bake for about 8 minutes, until lightly golden and no longer sticky. Put the cookies on a rack to cool and dry. They can be stored in an airtight container in a cool, dry place for several months.

Dark honey, such as carob or buckwheat ✖ 8 ounces/226 grams

00 flour ✖ 1¼ cups (5 ounces/142 grams)

ugly but delicious

Brutti ma buoni

MAKES 1 DOZEN

REGION: Piedmont, with versions throughout northern Italy

Crunchy on the outside, soft and chewy on the inside, these "ugly" cookies are so good that almost every region of Italy has its own version. Feel free to substitute almonds or walnuts for the hazelnuts, if you like. In some parts of Italy the batter may include a little grated orange peel, a bit of vanilla, or pinch of cinnamon.

Chopped hazelnuts ✳ 1½ cups (6 ounces/ 170 grams)

Sugar ✳ ¾ cup (5 ½ ounces/150 grams)

Egg whites ✳ 3 large

Preheat the oven to 280°F (140°C). Line a baking sheet with parchment paper.

Grind the hazelnuts and sugar in a mini food processor to a sandlike consistency. Don't overgrind or you'll create hazelnut butter.

In a small bowl, using a whisk or electric hand-mixer, beat the egg whites until firm peaks form.

Put the hazelnut-sugar mixture in a medium saucepan and fold in the egg whites. Cook over very low heat, stirring with a wooden spoon, for about 8 minutes, until thick. Remove from the heat and let the batter stand for 10 minutes.

Drop tablespoon-size dollops of the batter onto the prepared baking sheet. Bake for about 30 minutes, or until dry to the touch. Cool on a rack. These can be stored in an air-tight container for one month.

drunken crostini

Crostini ubriachi

SERVES 8 TO 10

REGION: Umbria

Like bread and chocolate, but boozy! Toasted baguette slices are dipped in melted chocolate that's been seasoned with espresso, rum, and liqueur. Then they're topped with more melted chocolate and almonds. Leave it to the Italians to create a wonderful no-bake, no-fuss, rich, chocolatey dessert from day-old bread.

Put 3 ounces (85 grams) of the milk chocolate and 1 ounce (30 grams) of the dark chocolate in a medium heatproof bowl and add the hot espresso. Stir until the chocolate melts. Add sugar, rum, and liqueur to taste, and stir to combine. Let cool completely.

Dip the toasted bread slices into the chocolate mixture, being sure to coat both sides, then place on a platter or other work surface and let rest for 1 hour so they can absorb the chocolate mixture.

Combine the remaining 2 ounces (55 grams) milk chocolate and 3 ounces (85 grams) dark chocolate in a small bowl and melt it, either in a microwave oven or over a saucepan of gently simmering water. Stir in the almonds until well combined, then spoon the mixture onto the crostini. Transfer the crostini to a serving platter and garnish with a generous sprinkle of chopped almonds.

Milk chocolate ✕ 5 ounces/140 grams, chopped

Dark chocolate ✕ 4 ounces/115 grams, chopped

Hot espresso or coffee ✕ ¾ cup (6 fluid ounces/180 milliliters)

Sugar

Rum ✕ 2 to 3 tablespoons

Liqueur such as amaretto, Maraschino, or *alchermes* (page 182) ✕ 2 to 3 tablespoons

1 day-old baguette, sliced 1-inch thick and toasted

Almonds ✕ ½ cup (2 ounces/55 grams), chopped, plus more for garnish

lemon-cornmeal cookies

Biscotti di meliga

MAKES 2 TO 3 DOZEN

REGION: Piedmont

In the Piedmontese dialect, *meliga* means "cornmeal"—and it is cornmeal that gives these cookies a rustic chewiness. The lemon adds a sophisticated bright, fresh tang. They are the quintessential cookies of Italy's northern regions and can be made in all sorts of shapes and sizes.

Fine-ground cornmeal ✕ 1 cup (5 ounces/ 140 grams)

00 flour ✕ ¾ cup (3 ounces/85 grams)

Butter, diced ✕ 10 tablespoons (5½ ounces/155 grams)

Sugar ✕ ¾ cup (5¼ ounces/150 grams)

Egg yolks ✕ 2 large

Pure vanilla extract ✕ 2 teaspoons

Grated zest of 1 large lemon

Salt

Preheat the oven to 350°F (180°C). Line two baking sheets with parchment paper.

In a food processor, combine the cornmeal, flour, and butter and process until the mixture resembles coarse sand. Add the sugar, egg yolks, vanilla, lemon zest, and salt and process until just combined. Turn the dough out onto a work surface and knead it for 1 to 2 minutes; the dough will be dense and sticky.

Working in batches, put the dough in a cookie press and press out simple one-part shapes onto the prepared baking sheets . Alternatively, put flattened teaspoon-sized mounds of dough on the prepared baking sheets.

Bake for about 7 minutes, depending on the thickness of your cookies, until just lightly golden at the edges. Let cool to room temperature on the parchment paper on wire racks. (If you try to remove them from the parchment paper before they are cool, they may crumble.) The cookies can be stored in an airtight container for several weeks.

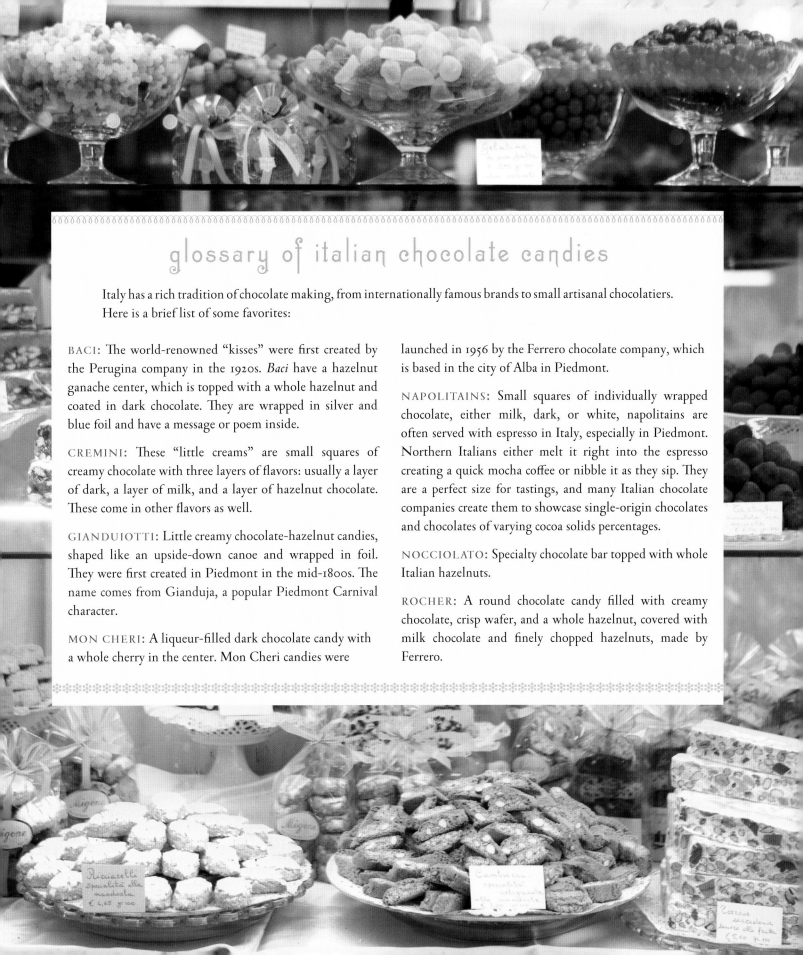

glossary of italian chocolate candies

Italy has a rich tradition of chocolate making, from internationally famous brands to small artisanal chocolatiers. Here is a brief list of some favorites:

BACI: The world-renowned "kisses" were first created by the Perugina company in the 1920s. *Baci* have a hazelnut ganache center, which is topped with a whole hazelnut and coated in dark chocolate. They are wrapped in silver and blue foil and have a message or poem inside.

CREMINI: These "little creams" are small squares of creamy chocolate with three layers of flavors: usually a layer of dark, a layer of milk, and a layer of hazelnut chocolate. These come in other flavors as well.

GIANDUIOTTI: Little creamy chocolate-hazelnut candies, shaped like an upside-down canoe and wrapped in foil. They were first created in Piedmont in the mid-1800s. The name comes from Gianduja, a popular Piedmont Carnival character.

MON CHERI: A liqueur-filled dark chocolate candy with a whole cherry in the center. Mon Cheri candies were launched in 1956 by the Ferrero chocolate company, which is based in the city of Alba in Piedmont.

NAPOLITAINS: Small squares of individually wrapped chocolate, either milk, dark, or white, napolitains are often served with espresso in Italy, especially in Piedmont. Northern Italians either melt it right into the espresso creating a quick mocha coffee or nibble it as they sip. They are a perfect size for tastings, and many Italian chocolate companies create them to showcase single-origin chocolates and chocolates of varying cocoa solids percentages.

NOCCIOLATO: Specialty chocolate bar topped with whole Italian hazelnuts.

ROCHER: A round chocolate candy filled with creamy chocolate, crisp wafer, and a whole hazelnut, covered with milk chocolate and finely chopped hazelnuts, made by Ferrero.

almond biscotti

Cantucci

MAKES ABOUT 2 DOZEN

REGION: Tuscany; first created in Siena, but now popular throughout Italy

I've taste-tested dozens of *cantucci* recipes, and this is my absolute favorite. The dough is very easy to work with and the cookies come out perfect every time. One key to the great flavor is the addition of *vin santo*, Tuscany's famed golden-amber dessert wine, which provides a nice aroma and a subtle fruity balance. Another is the touch of honey, which keeps the *cantucci* wonderfully moist.

00 flour ✕ 3 cups (13½ ounces/385 grams)

Sugar ✕ ¾ cup (5¼ ounces/150 grams)

Honey ✕ 3 heaping tablespoons

Eggs ✕ 2 large

Egg yolks ✕ 2 large

Butter ✕ 2 tablespoons

Baking powder ✕ ½ teaspoon

Vin santo ✕ ½ cup (4 fluid ounces/ 120 milliliters)

Salt ✕ ¼ teaspoon

Whole almonds ✕ 1 cup (5⅓ ounces/ 150 grams)

Preheat the oven to 350°F (180°C). Line a baking sheet with parchment paper.

In a large bowl, combine the flour, sugar, honey, whole eggs, egg yolks, butter, baking powder, *vin santo*, and salt. Using your hands, knead until a dough forms, then knead in the almonds. The dough should be a little sticky; if it's too moist, add a little extra flour.

Divide the dough into 3 portions and transfer them to the prepared baking sheet. Using wet hands, mold each portion into a log about 10 inches (25 centimeters) long and 2 inches (5 centimeters) wide. Don't worry about it being perfect—the dough will even out as it bakes.

Bake for 25 minutes, then remove from the oven but keep the oven on. Let the logs rest on the baking sheet for 5 minutes. While still hot, working directly on the baking sheet, cut the logs on the diagonal into slices about ¾ inches (2 centimeters) thick, using a sharp knife and one firm cut. Arrange the slices, cut side down, on the baking sheet and return them to the oven to bake for about 5 minutes, until light golden. Cool on wire racks. The biscotti can be stored in an airtight container for several months.

UN ALTRO MODO

Orange *Cantucci*: Add 2 to 3 tablespoons finely minced candied orange peel when you add the almonds to the dough.

Chocolate *Cantucci*: Add a small handful of chopped dark chocolate or mini dark chocolate chips when you add the almonds to the dough.

Anything-Goes *Cantucci*: Add a few tablespoons of chopped dried fruit—like dates, apricots, or figs—and substitute a different nut for the almonds, or omit the nuts.

corsini, traditional tuscan bakers

When I last visited Tuscany, I tried lots of the region's sweets, including *cantucci, panforte, ricciardelli,* and *pandesanti.* Almost invariably, when I found an especially delicious example and asked who made it, I was told, "Corsini." I had to track down the company that made so many of my favorite Tuscan cookies! As it turns out, it's not so much a company as it is a family: a man and his four sons, who manage a little factory so picturesque, so idyllic, I found it hard to believe it was real. The factory is really more like a series of small bake shops, each staffed by a small group of people dedicated to producing a different sweet. In one room, workers take two-hour shifts carefully picking out almonds not quite beautiful enough to feature in the Corsini *cantucci.* (The rejects, still sound but perhaps a little misshapen, are ground up and used in other products.) The factory's quaintness and the personal touches like this that can be seen throughout the operation are all the more surprising since Corsini is a very big name in Europe. The company's sweets are found throughout Italy, and their teatime cookies are among the most popular brands in England. Corsini even makes the biscotti for European Starbucks.

This small factory is part of the tiny Tuscan hilltop town of Castel del Piano, which is surrounded by pristine rustic countryside that could've emerged, shaded in deep greens and umber, from a da Vinci painting. It's the same town where Ubaldo Corsini first started working at his father's bread shop, established in 1921. After his father, Corrado Corsini, passed away in 1957, Ubaldo took over. At the time he was just eighteen, but he made the most of the business. Ubaldo loved all sweets. After he took over the bakery, he slowly incorporated more and more sweet breads and different kinds of cookies, and eventually chose to focus exclusively on sweets. As soon as his sons were old enough and showed an interest in helping him, they worked together to grow the company. And grow it did: The business has increased twenty-fold.

Ubaldo, still president of the company, claims he's twelve pounds (5.5 kilograms) overweight because he's the "official taste-tester."

"Like many typical Italian families," Ubaldo says, "we don't know where the family ends and the business begins."

hazelnut-chocolate kisses

Baci di dama

MAKES ABOUT 3 DOZEN

REGION: Piedmont

A dab of rich dark chocolate sandwiched between two buttery hazelnut domes, this little kiss of a cookie, aptly named *baci di dama*, which means "a lady's kisses," will melt in your mouth. The simple four-ingredient dough comes together right in the food processor.

Preheat the oven to 350°F (180°C). Line two baking sheets with parchment paper and set aside.

Combine the hazelnuts and 2 tablespoons of the sugar in a food processor and process until finely ground. Add the remaining sugar, sift in the flour, and process until well combined. Add the butter and pulse until combined. The dough will be a dense mass. Divide the dough in half, shape into disks, wrap in plastic wrap, and refrigerate for at least 2 hours, until very firm and cold.

Unwrap one disk of dough (leave the other in the refrigerator so it stays cold). Pinch off a teaspoonful of the dough and roll it into a small ball, about the size of a hazelnut, a little less than 1/2 inch (12 millimeters) in diameter. Occasionally flour your hands so the dough doesn't get too sticky as it warms in your hands. (The key to nicely rounded cookies is a fairly dry dough.) Place the balls on a prepared baking sheet at least 2 inches (5 centimeters) apart. Put the filled baking sheet in the refrigerator while you repeat with the second disk of dough. Be sure to make an even number of balls, as you'll need two to make one *baci*.

When both cookie sheets are filled, bake for about 13 minutes, until just light golden. Keeping the cookies on the parchment paper, slide them off the baking sheets and onto a cool surface to stop them from cooking further. Let them cool to room temperature before filling.

Put the chocolate in a small bowl and melt it, either in a microwave oven or over a saucepan of gently simmering water. To make the kisses, put a dollop of chocolate on the flat side (the side that had been touching the baking sheet) of one cookie and then make a sandwich by pressing another cookie onto the chocolate. Repeat with all the cookies. The cookies can be stored in an airtight container in a cool, dry place for several weeks.

dammi mille baci,
poi cento, poi mille altri,
poi ancora cento...

GIVE ME A THOUSAND KISSES, THEN A HUNDRED, THEN A THOUSAND MORE, AND ANOTHER HUNDRED...
—GAIUS VALERIUS CATULLUS, ROMAN POET (1ST CENTURY B.C.)

Whole blanched hazelnuts ✕ 7/8 cup (3½ ounces/100 grams), oven toasted

Sugar ✕ 1/2 cup (3½ ounces/100 grams)

All-purpose flour ✕ 3/4 cup (3½ ounces/100 grams)

Butter, diced ✕ 7 tablespoons (3½ ounces/100 grams)

Dark chocolate, chopped ✕ 3½ ounces/100 grams

UN ALTRO MODO

Chocolate-Chocolate *Baci di Dama:* Substitute 2 tablespoons unsweetened cocoa powder for 2 tablespoons of the flour when you make the dough.

chocolate-almond honey bars

Mostaccioli al cioccolato

MAKES ABOUT 2 DOZEN

REGION: Calabria

These bar cookies feature a magically moist chocolate and almond filling surrounded by honey-rich dough. If you like honey, especially the more intense and flavorful dark kinds, these cookies are for you. I love them not just for the taste, but also for the technique. The dough and filling are baked as you would a pie, then cut into individual bars. I also like that there's no butter in the recipe, allowing more of the naturally rich almond and chocolate flavors to come through.

Olive oil for the pan

00 flour ✕ 2 cups (9 ounces/255 grams)

Dark honey, such as chestnut or buckwheat ✕ about ¾ cup (8 ounces/227 grams)

Egg yolk ✕ 1 large

Baking powder ✕ 1 teaspoon

Dark chocolate, melted ✕ 11 ounces/ 310 grams

Whole almonds, oven toasted and finely ground ✕ 1 cup (5⅓ ounces/150 grams)

Preheat the oven to 350°F (180°C). Lightly oil and flour a 10-inch (25-centimeter) pie pan.

In a large bowl, stir together the flour, honey, egg yolk, and baking powder until a dough forms. It will be very sticky. Put a sheet of parchment paper on a work surface and lightly dust it with flour. Take a little more than half of the dough and roll it out into a circle at least 12 inches (25 centimeters) in diameter so it will line the pie pan up to the top edge. The dough is very sticky, so it may not easily come off the parchment paper in one piece. Just press the pieces together in the pie pan; they will come together when the pie bakes. Roll the rest of the dough out into a circle for the top crust on the same sheet of parchment paper and set it aside.

In a small bowl, stir together the chocolate and almonds until well blended. Pour into the pie pan and cover with the top crust. Pinch the edges closed so that they just touch, creating a flush edge. Do not crimp the edges as in typical American pies. Bake for about 15 minutes, until the crust is lightly golden. Let cool to room temperature on a wire rack, then cut into roughly rectangular bars. The bars can be stored in an airtight container for up to 1 month.

Vanilla cookies

Ovis mollis

MAKES ABOUT 3 DOZEN

REGION: Throughout Italy, especially in the north

essere pieno come un uovo.

FULL AS AN EGG.

I asked Giancarlo Gonizzi, the curator of the outstanding cookbook collection at Academia Barilla in Parma, for his advice on a must-include dessert for this book. He suggested these cookies, which come from one of Italy's most famed dessert books, the 1927 classic *Il Pasticcere e Confettiere Moderno* written by Giuseppe Ciocca.

Moist and versatile, they contain two unusual ingredients: cooked egg yolks and cornstarch. That combination yields an exceptionally tender cookie with exceptionally silky mouthfeel.

They can be made in almost any shape, but I like them as thumbprints, filled with jam or melted chocolate.

Hard-cooked egg yolks × 5 large

Sugar × 1/2 cup (3 1/2 ounces/100 grams)

Butter × 14 tablespoons (7 ounces/200 grams)

Cornstarch × 3/4 cup (3 ounces/85 grams)

Pure vanilla extract × 1 teaspoon

All-purpose flour × 1 1/2 cups (7 ounces/198 grams)

Confectioners' sugar, jam, or melted chocolate

Preheat the oven to 325°F (165°C). Line two baking sheets with parchment paper.

Combine the cooked egg yolks and granulated sugar in a food processor and process until smooth. Add the butter and process until creamy. Add the cornstarch and vanilla, then the flour, pulsing until just combined. Do not overwork the dough.

Pinch off bits of the dough and roll them into 1/2-inch (12-millimeter) balls. Place on the prepared baking sheets and press down gently in the center of each ball with your thumb. Place the filled baking sheets in the refrigerator for 10 minutes to firm up the dough, then bake for about 20 minutes, until the cookies are dry to the touch. They will be light colored. Cool to room temperature on the baking sheets without handling them, as the cookies are very fragile when hot. Serve as they are, or dust with confectioners' sugar or fill the thumbprints with jam or chocolate.

Venice's cornmeal cookies

Zaleti

MAKES ABOUT 2 DOZEN

REGION: Veneto

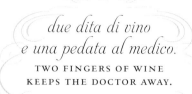

There are some terrific foodie websites and bloggers in Italy. One question I sent out into Italy's cyberspace was which cookie recipes I should include in this book. Almost unanimously, Italian bloggers agreed that I had to include *zaleti*—cornmeal cookies from the Veneto region. *Zaletti* means "yellow" in Veneto dialect, which refers to the cookie's cornmeal color. After trying several recipes sent to me by various chefs and home cooks, this is the standout. The hint of grappa gives these cookies a subtle but sublime aroma.

Butter ✳ 8 tablespoons (4 ounces/113 grams)

Sugar ✳ ½ cup (3½ ounces/100 grams)

Egg yolks ✳ 3 large

Milk ✳ 4 tablespoons

Baking powder ✳ 1 teaspoon

Salt ✳ ½ teaspoon

Grated zest of 1 lemon

Pure vanilla extract ✳ 1 teaspoon

Grappa ✳ 2 tablespoons

1 handful of golden raisins

Pine nuts ✳ 3 tablespoons

Fine-ground cornmeal ✳ 1 cup (5 ounces/140 grams)

00 flour ✳ 1½ cups (6 ounces/170 grams)

Confectioners' sugar

Preheat the oven to 375°F (190°C). Line two baking sheets with parchment paper.

With an electric mixer fitted with the whisk attachment, beat the butter and granulated sugar until light yellow and fluffy. Beat in the egg yolks until well combined, then beat in the milk, baking powder, salt, lemon zest, vanilla, and grappa (if using). With a wooden spoon, stir in the raisins and pine nuts. Gradually sift in the cornmeal and flour, a little at a time, incorporating each addition well before adding more. The dough will be very dense. Drop the heaping tablespoons of the dough onto the prepared baking sheets a few inches apart. Bake for 12 to 14 minutes, until just light golden around the edges. Do not overbake. Cool to room temperature on wire racks.

Dust with confectioners' sugar and serve. The cookies can be stored in an airtight container for up to a month.

black pepper–honey biscotti

Pepatelli

MAKES 8 DOZEN

REGION: Abruzzo, especially the Teramo area

Honey-sweet, with a pleasing peppery bite and hint of orange, these thin, crunchy biscotti are positively addictive. Best of all, they're a guiltless treat! Unlike most cookies, these contain no butter or eggs. The absurdly simple list of ingredients—basically just honey, almonds, and flour—produces a very sophisticated cookie, especially wonderful when made with a strongly flavored darker honey like chestnut or buckwheat.

The yield might sound like a lot, but these cookies are very, very thin. *Pepatelli* are typically served in the winter, especially for the holidays, enjoyed with a glass of the local Abruzzo dessert wine, *vin cotto*. The basic recipe—without the relatively modern addition of cocoa powder—dates to the Renaissance.

Preheat the oven to 350°F (180°C). Line a baking sheet with parchment paper.

In a microwave oven or in a small saucepan over low heat, heat the honey until very warm and liquidy. Pour into a medium bowl and add the almonds, flour, orange zest, cocoa powder, and pepper. Mix, using your hands or a wooden spoon, until a dough forms. It will be very dense and crumbly. Don't worry; it will come together as it bakes.

Put a little flour in a small bowl or on a work surface and coat your hands with it. Put one quarter of the dough on the prepared baking sheet and press it into a rectangle ¾-inch (2-centimeters) thick, about 6 inches (15 centimeters) long and 1½ inches (4 centimeters) wide. Repeat with the remaining dough to make a total of 4 rectangles.

Bake for 10 minutes. Flip the rectangles over and bake for another 15 minutes, or until golden and set.

Remove from the oven and, while still hot, cut each rectangle crosswise into very thin slices, about ¼ inch (6 millimeters) thick. Cool to room temperature on wire racks. The cookies can be stored in an airtight container for several months.

Honey ✖ 9 ounces (250 grams)

Whole almonds ✖ 1½ cups (9 ounces/250 grams)

00 flour ✖ 1¾ cups (9 ounces/250 grams)

Grated zest of 1 orange

Unsweetened cocoa powder ✖ 1 teaspoon

Freshly ground black pepper ✖ 1 teaspoon

red wine rings

Tarallucci al vino

MAKES ABOUT 7 DOZEN

REGION: Abruzzo

*tutto finisce a
tarallucci e vino.*

IT ALL ENDS WITH TARALLUCCI
AND WINE. (IT ALL COMES OUT
RIGHT IN THE END.)

Attention, red wine lovers: This is the perfect dessert for you! Not only do these treats pair perfectly with red wine, but they're made with it, too. These ring-shaped cookies have long been seen by Italians as symbolizing a hug, and are a sign of friendship and affection. In the past, when legal contracts were made—such as for the sale of land—villagers didn't employ lawyers. Instead they'd simply shake hands and embrace. To celebrate they'd offer a toast of red wine and *tarallucci*. Today, these cookies come out after dinner, to be nibbled on while drinking the last of the wine.

Made with olive oil and not too sweet, they're a guiltless pleasure. Seven dozen may sound like a lot—and you can halve the recipe if you like—but you won't regret making a full batch. For one thing, they are a snap to make and will stay fresh for months. For another, when you serve them to guests, they'll beg to take some home. *Tarallucci al vino* are a wonderful hostess gift for the wine lovers in your life.

All-purpose flour ✕ 7 cups (35 ounces/
1 kilogram)

Red wine ✕ 1 cup (8 fluid ounces/
240 milliliters)

Sugar ✕ 1 cup (7 ounces/200 grams)

Olive oil ✕ ¾ cup (6 fluid ounces/
180 milliliters)

Eggs ✕ 2 large

Salt ✕ ½ teaspoon

in italy

This recipe is common throughout Italy, with slight variations in size and name. In Basilicata and southern Italy, you will find a larger version called *taralli*, which are boiled before baking. In Rome and central Italy, a similar cookie is called *ciambelline al vino*.

Preheat the oven to 350°F (180°C). Line two baking sheets with parchment paper.

In a large bowl, combine the flour, the wine, sugar, oil, eggs, and salt, using your fingers or a wooden spoon. Add more flour, a little at a time, until a firm dough forms.

Put a few tablespoons sugar on a small flat plate. Put a sheet of parchment paper on a work surface and roll a large handful of dough into a long rope about ½ inch (12 millimeters) wide. Cut off a 3-inch (7.5-centimeter) section and shape it into a ring, pinching the ends to seal it. Dip one side of each cookie into the sugar and put it, sugar side up, on one of the prepared baking sheets. Repeat to fill one baking sheet (see Note). Bake for about 15 minutes, until dry to the touch. Cool on wire racks while you shape and bake the remaining *tarallucci*. The *tarallucci* can be stored in an airtight container in a cool, dry place for up to 3 months.

NOTE: I learned a great trick from an Italian friend. As soon as you have shaped one baking sheet's worth of *tarallucci*, pop them in the oven so they can bake while you're forming the next batch. In the few minutes it'll take you to fill the second baking sheet, you'll be rewarded with a taste from the first.

UN ALTRO MODO

Instead of sprinkling the *tarallucci* with sugar before baking, you can instead glaze them with icing. Just add a few drops of water to confectioners' sugar in a shallow bowl, and stir until a thin icing forms. After they are baked and cooled, dip the top half of each *tarallucci* in the icing and let dry.

glossary of italian cookies

Although there are probably hundreds of different cookies and recipe variations to be found across the country, here are some of the most popular:

AMARETTI: *Amaretti,* "little bitters," are small, round almond cookies. A speciality of northern Italy, *amaretti* are made of sugar, almonds, and egg whites. Their invention is attributed to Francesco Moriondo, pastry chef at the court of Savoy in the mid-seventeenth century.

Amaretti can be either hard (*classici*) or soft (*morbidi*), and can vary in size, too. Hard *amaretti* are used in many traditional Italian recipes, from savory dishes to desserts. In desserts they are often a base for custard (page 72), *semifreddo,* and cake decorations (pages 126). In savory dishes, they are famously the filling for pumpkin ravioli and tortellini.

BACI DI DAMA (page 21): *Baci di dama,* "lady's kisses," are a specialty of Piedmont in northern Italy. Two little round hazelnut-almond shortbread cookies are sandwiched together with a dark chocolate filling.

CANESTRELLI: *Canestrelli,* "little baskets," are ring-shaped, frilly-edged shortbread or almond biscuits topped with confectioners' sugar after baking. *Canestrelli* originated in the Monferrato area, between the regions of Piedmont and Liguria.

CANTUCCI: (page 18) also called *biscotti di Prato,* are crunchy almond cookies first created in the Tuscan town of Prato centuries ago. *Cantuccini* are smaller-sized *cantucci.* They are traditionally served with a glass of *vin santo,* an amber-colored dessert wine.

CAVALLUCCI: *Cavallucci,* "little horses," are soft cookies made with honey, nuts, and anise and are eaten all year round in Siena, but in the rest of Italy mostly at Christmastime. They date back to the Middle Ages in Siena, and the name probably comes from the tradition of offering them to travelers at the stables of area inns.

CROCCANTE: *Croccante,* "crunchy," are crisp nutty sweets that are a cross between a cookie and a candy. They can be made with all sorts of nuts. Pistachio *croccante* are a specialty of Sicily, which is renowned for its Bronte pistachios.

FAVE DEI MORTI: *Fave dei morti,* "dead man's beans," are bean-shaped cookies made with almonds, pine nuts, and egg whites. They are traditionally eaten on November 1st for All Soul's Day and originated in the Umbria and Lombardy regions of Italy.

KRUMIRI OR CRUMIRI: *Krumiri* were created in Casale Monferrato, a small town in Piedmont, as tribute to Vittorio Emanuele II (1820–1878), the first king of Italy. Made of flour, butter, and honey, their shape is thought to be based on the king's handlebar mustache.

RICCIARELLI: Originating in Siena in the Middle Ages, *ricciarelli,* "curly," are soft oval-shaped cookies. They are made with ground almonds, sugar, honey, and egg whites and topped with confectioners' sugar or chocolate. *Ricciarelli* are associated with the feast of the Annunciation (March 25) but are eaten all year long. The recipe for *ricciarelli* is one of Italy's oldest. The cookie is documented as having been served on numerous important historic occasions dating back to the fifteenth century.

SAVOIARDI: *Savoiardi,* known as ladyfingers in the United States, were first created in the Piedmont region in 1348, during the early Renaissance, for the royal Savoia family—hence the cookie's name. *Savoiardi* recipes are cited in several historic Italian cookbooks, including Bartolomeo Stefani's *Art of Good Cooking,* published in 1662. Because Italian-made *savoiardi* soak up liquid so nicely, they are a key ingredient in hundreds of desserts, including charlottes, puddings, refrigerator cakes (page 75), and, of course, tiramisù (pages 131 and 133). This cookie is so important to Italians that the recipe is regulated and the name protected.

SFOGLIATELLE: *Sfogliatelle,* "little sheets," are a flaky, fan-shaped pastry filled with either pastry custard or sweetened ricotta and semolina flour. A specialty of Naples, *sfogliatelle* are eaten mainly for breakfast and not as an after-meal dessert.

cannoli

MAKES ABOUT 16

REGION: Sicily

*figliuole e frittelle:
quante più se ne fa,
più vengon belle.*

CHILDREN AND FRIED FOOD:
THE MORE YOU MAKE, THE BETTER
THEY COME OUT.

Cannoli, deep-fried tubes of dough filled with sweetened ricotta, are the quintessential Sicilian dessert. I'll be the first to admit that homemade cannoli shells are tricky to make! For the most part, not even Sicilian grandmas make them anymore. That said, I've experimented with several recipes, and this one is a keeper. Follow the directions and you'll get a nice crunchy shell. Maybe not on the first one, but, as the saying goes, the more you make, the better they'll look. You'll be a pro by mid-batch.

The filling is delicious, and simple as can be. If you're at all wary about making your own shells, make a deconstructed cannoli! Luigi Falanga, owner of Sabra, an artisan cookie company in Sicily, showed me how he serves cannoli filling on a plate accompanied by his crisp, crunchy pistachio *croccante* cookies to scoop it up.

FOR THE FILLING (SEE NOTE):

Ricotta cheese ✳ 2 cups (1 pound/455 grams)

Superfine sugar ✳ 4 tablespoons

Mini chocolate chips or finely chopped dark chocolate ✳ 2 to 3 tablespoons

Candied citron or candied orange peel, finely minced ✳ 2 to 3 tablespoons, optional

Make the filling: Combine the ricotta and sugar in a bowl and mash with a wooden spoon until smooth and creamy. Cover with plastic wrap and refrigerate for 24 hours. Pass the mixture through a food mill or fine-mesh sieve, then stir in the chocolate and candied citron (if using) and refrigerate until ready to use.

Make the shells: In a large bowl, using your fingers, mix together the flour, lard, sugar, cocoa powder, and salt until the lard is incorporated into the flour. Add the egg yolk (reserve the egg white for later), vinegar, and Marsala and mix until a firm dough forms. Add more Marsala, just a few drops at a time, if the dough is too dry, or more flour if the dough is too moist. Knead the dough until it is very smooth. You can do this by hand or you can pass the dough through a pasta machine several times. Wrap the dough in plastic wrap and refrigerate for 2 hours.

Roll out the dough until it is very thin (about $1/10$ inch/2.5 millimeters thick), using a rolling pin or by passing it once again through a pasta machine. If using a pasta machine, divide the dough in half and pass one of the halves through the pasta machine a few times, until you can pass it through the middle-sized opening to create a long, thin sheet of dough. Cover the sheet of dough with plastic wrap and repeat with the remaining dough.

Using a cookie cutter, or working freehand with a sharp knife, cut the dough into roughly 4-inch (10-centimeter) ovals or rectangles to fit 5-inch- (12.5-centimeters) diameter metal cannoli tubes.

Use a deep fryer, or heat about 2 inches (5 centimeters) oil in a small, heavy-bottomed pan over medium heat. You can test to see if the oil is hot enough by putting a tiny piece of dough into the hot oil. If it rises to the top fairly quickly, the oil is hot enough.

Lightly oil the outside of the cannoli tubes. Wrap an oval around a tube and brush the edge of the dough with a little egg white at the point where the edges will overlap. Press firmly to seal. Repeat with the remaining tubes. Fry the tubes, a few at a time, turning them gently, until golden on all sides, about 3 to 4 minutes total. Transfer to a paper towel–lined plate to drain. Turn them so that they drain completely. Carefully remove the shells from the hot tube and, once the tubes have cooled, repeat with the remaining dough. The cannoli shells can be stored in an airtight container for up to 2 days.

Put filling into each shell, either with a piping bag or using a small spoon and putting some in through one end and some through the other end. Garnish the exposed filling, if you like, with candied fruit, pistachios, or chocolate chips, and dust the top of the pastry with confectioners' sugar. Serve within 1 hour of filling.

NOTE: The secret to really great cannoli filling is to let the ricotta and sugar mixture rest in the refrigerator overnight—preferably 24 hours. This lets the sugar dissolve and combine smoothly with the cheese to create that lush mouthfeel. Another plus: This technique allows you to use less sugar. You may be tempted to muscle your way through and blend the ricotta and sugar with an electric hand mixer to get it creamy, but don't. You'll risk having a watery ricotta, and you'll need to add more sugar to thicken it.

You will need special metal cannoli tubes, about ½ by 5-inches, which are available online, through Amazon, Chef Tools, and other suppliers of kitchen equipment, or in specialty gourmet shops.

FOR THE SHELLS:

00 flour ✻ 2 cups (9 ounces/255 grams)

Lard or butter ✻ 2 tablespoons

Sugar ✻ 3 tablespoons

Unsweetened cocoa powder ✻ 2 teaspoons; or ground cinnamon ✻ ¼ teaspoon

Salt ✻ ¼ teaspoon

Egg ✻ 1 large, separated

Distilled white vinegar ✻ 2 teaspoons

Marsala wine ✻ 3 tablespoons

Sunflower or vegetable oil for frying

OPTIONAL FINISHING TOUCHES:

Candied fruit such as citron, cherries, or orange peel, chopped pistachios, or chocolate chips

Confectioners' sugar

in italy

Although originally eaten only during Carnival, now cannoli are enjoyed year round throughout Italy. As Carnival celebrations are traditionally bawdy, the naturally phallic shape of cannoli is exaggerated by making extra-jumbo-sized ones, called *cannolone*.

According to Sicilian tradition, when you offer cannoli to guests, there have to be at least twelve on the serving plate. Interestingly, in the *Smorfia Napoletana,* a series of numbers given by the reading of dreams to play the Lotto, the number thirty-four is called *il Cannolo* and signifies that you'll soon get good news.

sweet ricotta crêpes

Dita degli apostoli

SERVES 6

REGION: Puglia

quattro "g" vuole il formaggio: grande, grasso, grave, e gratis dato.

CHEESE IS BEST WITH FOUR GS: GRAND, GREASY, GREAT, AND GIVEN FOR FREE.

"Apostles' fingers," as they're called in Italy, is a weird name for a delicious dessert. If you like cannoli, you'll love these. They're made with the same sort of filling, but served in crêpes instead of fried tubes. The crêpes—flourless, light, and very aromatic—are also terrific simply spread with Nutella or crema gianduia.

Ricotta cheese ✼ 1½ cups (12 ounces/ 340 grams)

Sugar ✼ ½ cup (3½ ounces/100 grams)

Dark chocolate ✼ 1½ ounces/40 grams, grated on a cheese grater

Aromatic liqueur or wine, such as limoncello, Strega, or Marsala ✼ 3 tablespoons

Eggs ✼ 4 large

Milk ✼ 4 tablespoons

Pinch of salt

Butter for the pan

Confectioners' sugar

UN ALTRO MODO

Add any of the following to the ricotta filling, if you like: 1 tablespoon minced candied orange peel or zest of ¼ orange or ½ lemon; 3 tablespoons brandied cherries, chopped, plus some of the liquid; or a pinch of ground cinnamon.

Press the ricotta and granulated sugar through a fine-mesh sieve into a medium bowl. Add the chocolate and 1 tablespoon of the liqueur and, using a fork, mix until well combined. Refrigerate for 1 to 2 hours so it thickens and the flavors combine.

In another medium bowl, using a whisk or an electric hand-mixer, beat together the eggs, milk, the remaining 2 tablespoons liqueur, and salt until well combined. Let rest for 30 minutes.

Lightly butter a 12-inch (30.5-centimeter) nonstick sauté pan and place it over medium heat. Pour about a third of the batter into the center of the pan and swirl the pan to spread the batter evenly. Cook on one side just until dry on top, then gently turn the crêpe over and cook the other side; remove to a cutting board. Repeat with the remaining batter, lightly buttering the pan before adding the batter for each crêpe. You should get three 12-inch (30.5-centimeter) crêpes, which, when cut, will yield 10 to 12 *dita* (or "fingers") per crêpe. Let cool to room temperature, then stack the crêpes on the board.

Cut the crêpes, one at a time, into 3-inch- (7.5 centimeters) wide strips: You'll have 4 long strips and 2 smaller end pieces (discard or snack on the end pieces). Cut the 4 longer sections in half crosswise. Put a heaping tablespoon of the filling onto each strip, spread it evenly, and roll into small fingers. The edges stay open, just like a jelly roll.

Arrange on a platter, cover with plastic wrap, and refrigerate for at least 30 minutes, until cold and firm, before serving. Serve topped with a light sprinkle of confectioners' sugar.

falanga-sabra, sicilian cookie maker

"Taste!" commanded my Italian journalist friend, handing me a cookie as we navigated the vastness of Cibus, Parma's prestigious fancy food show. "This just won the Cibus 2008's *Vassoio d'Oro* prize for *il miglior nuovo prodotto dolciario dell'anno*—the best new dessert product of the year! It's made by Falanga-Sabra, a Sicilian company."

Even before taking a bite of the pretty pistachio-studded flat square, I'm hit with the aroma of roasted nuts and caramelized sugar. And the flavor? A cross between nut brittle and butter cookie. Crunchy but not dry, sweet but not too sweet, and full of pistachio flavor. Sicilian pistachios are unmistakable, and these are fabulous.

My friend introduced me to the company's owner, Luigi Falanga, a charming and energetic gentleman whose passion for Sicily and its sweets was so compelling that right then and there I asked if I might schedule a tour of his facility for my next trip to Italy. Months later, I made my visit to Catania. Entering the workroom, I am enveloped by the mouthwatering aromas of sugar, citrus fruit, and roasting nuts. Several bakers are busy mixing batter and baking cookies in small batches, and soon I am transported to my childhood, to my nonna's house, when she would gather all my cousins into the kitchen to help her bake during the holidays.

Luigi hands me a small round lemon-almond cookie, made with Sicily's renowned lemons, fresh from the oven. Ambrosia! What makes these so good? I nibble as he explains the premise behind his cookies: "I wanted to create old-fashioned cookies, featuring only the very best all-natural Sicilian ingredients—lemons, pistachios, almonds, oranges, and honey—but to make them in a more modern size and shape and with less sugar." Falanga's mission is personal. His grandfather was a pastry chef, and every afternoon after school he'd visit his nonno's shop, where he absorbed a philosophy that stayed with him: "Only bake with a soul that is happy and full of love." Years later, by then a successful financial consultant, Luigi still harbored a dream: to follow in his grandfather's confectionery footsteps and in the process reinvigorate Sicilian cookies and pastries. In 1997, he quit finance completely and founded his confectionery, Falanga, la Pasticceria Siciliana. He spent two more years testing and refining his products.

Today, Falanga's Sabra products number in the dozens, available not just in shops and hotels in Sicily but at select outlets around the United States, too. In addition to the award-winning pistachio-almond *croccante*, the company's signature cookie offerings include Almond "*stelle*," "*rose*," and "*gocce*" (stars, roses, and drops), two kinds of butter cookies, hazelnut *gocce*, chocolate *gocce*, and many more. All are individually seal-wrapped immediately after baking, so even though they're preservative-free their shelf-life is quite long and well suited for export.

Luigi Falanga's enthusiasm is infectious. He is a man who has methodically chosen to follow his heart—and it guided him straight back to the warmest memories of his childhood. To him, "It is a delight to follow in my family's pastry tradition, which is also such a strong Sicilian tradition. My mission is to use artisan craftsmanship in creating our cookies, and employ industrial techniques only for the nonedible aspects of the business—packing, shipping, and the like. This marriage between artisanal and industrial allows our company the honor of being able to export the best of Sicily's sweets around the world."

sicilian sesame cookies

Biscotti regina

MAKES 2 DOZEN

REGION: **Sicily**

A Sicilian classic! A satisfyingly moist, lemony center encased in a crunchy sesame-seed crust. This is a bullet-proof recipe that produces pastry shop–perfect cookies every time.

The various names for these cookies run the gamut, from the elegant *biscotti regina*, "queen's cookie," to the comical *strunzi di sciocca*, "chicken's poop," to the slightly irreverent *strunzi d'ancilu*, "angel's poop."

In a large bowl, combine the flour, sugar, and butter until the mixture resembles coarse sand. Add the egg yolks, milk, honey, lemon zest, and salt and knead until a dough forms. Roll the dough into a ball, cover with plastic wrap, and refrigerate for at least 1 hour.

Preheat the oven to 350°F (180°C). Line a baking sheet with parchment paper. Toast the sesame seeds in a dry skillet until light golden. Set aside in a shallow bowl or plate.

In a small bowl, using a fork, beat the egg whites with 3 tablespoons water. Divide the chilled dough into 4 portions. Roll each section out into a log about 1 inch (2.5 centimeters) thick. Cut the log into 1½-inch (4-centimeter) sections.

Dip each section in the egg whites, then roll in the sesame seeds, covering all sides, and place on the prepared baking sheet. Bake for 30 minutes, until golden. Cool on a wire rack. The cookies can be stored in an airtight container for several weeks.

NOTE: Butter or oil will give these cookies a softer center, while lard will make them crunchier.

All-purpose flour ✖ 2 cups (12 ounces/350 grams)

Sugar ✖ ½ cup (3½ ounces/100 grams)

Butter, olive oil, or lard ✖ 8 tablespoons (4 ounces/115 grams)

Eggs ✖ 3 large, separated

Milk ✖ 2 tablespoons

Honey ✖ 1 tablespoon

Grated zest of ½ lemon

Salt ✖ ¼ teaspoon

Sesame seeds ✖ ¾ cup (3½ ounces/100 grams)

chocolate and jam "little mouthfuls"

Bocconotti

MAKES ABOUT 3 DOZEN

REGION: Abruzzo, Calabria, and Lazio

Filled with chocolate, ground almonds, and grape jam, these tiny, two-bite mini pies have an intriguing combination of flavors.

If the idea of making piecrust seems daunting, you'll love this recipe. Unlike most dough for pies and tarts, this one doesn't require rolling or chilling and is just pressed into molds. Made with olive oil, not butter, these mini pies are healthy as well as tasty.

Like so many dishes in Italy, *bocconotti* vary from region to region. This recipe is from Abruzzo, where they are filled with either a cooked reduced dessert wine called "*vin cotto*" or with a jam made from the local exquisite Montelpuciano grapes. In Calabria, they are filled instead with just marmalade, and in the Lazio region, with sweetened ricotta.

Egg yolks ✕ 6 large

Sugar ✕ ½ cup (3½ ounces/100 grams)

Olive or other vegetable oil ✕ ½ cup (4 fluid ounces/120 milliliters)

Pure vanilla extract ✕ ½ teaspoon

Grated zest of 1 lemon

All-purpose flour ✕ 1⅞ cups (8 ounces/225 grams)

Grape Jam (page 202) or store-bought ✕ ¾ cup (6 fluid ounces/180 milliliters)

Almond flour or very finely ground blanched almonds ✕ ⅓ cup (1⅔ ounces/45 grams)

Dark chocolate ✕ 2 ounces/55 grams, grated on a cheese grater

Pinch of ground cinnamon

Preheat the oven to 350°F (180°C).

In a medium bowl, combine the egg yolks and sugar and beat with an electric mixer until golden yellow and creamy. Add the oil, vanilla, and half of the lemon zest and beat until combined. Gradually add the flour, mixing until a dough forms. Set aside.

In another medium bowl, combine the jam, almond flour, chocolate, cinnamon, and remaining lemon zest and stir until well combined.

Lightly oil 36 mini muffin cups or 2-inch (5 centimeters) tart molds. Press about 1 rounded tablespoon of the dough into the bottom of each mold. Top with a heaping tablespoon of the jam mixture. Take another tablespoon of the dough and press it flat with your palms. Top the filling with the disk of dough and press it into the edges of the mold to seal. Sprinkle with sugar. Bake until golden, about 20 minutes.

spiked rice pudding treats

Torta degli addobbi

SERVES 10

REGION: Emilia-Romagna, especially Bologna

Today, this is one of the most popular homemade desserts of northern Italy, making an appearance at virtually every potluck, birthday, and office party.

A quick glance at the list of ingredients and you'd think this is just another rice pudding recipe, but it's not! Although it does start out as rice pudding, it's jazzed up with rum, almonds, and citrus, baked, and then topped with almond liqueur, which creates a tasty glaze. Finally it's cooled, cut into bite-sized diamond shapes and, as is tradition, served with toothpicks. The result is a fabulous sort of a rice pudding "cookie."

This dessert takes its name from the *Festa degli Addobbi,* a religious festival that takes place in late spring in Bologna. *Addobbare* means to decorate or dressup and, during the festival, religious statues are paraded through town. In the past, parishioners would decorate windows and balconies with flowers, wreaths, banners, and other adornments and invite neighbors from nearby parishes to the celebration. *Torta degli addobbi* would be served, with each parish vying for best recipe.

In a large saucepan over medium heat, combine the milk, sugar, lemon zest, and salt and bring to a low boil. Add the rice, stirring to combine. Bring to a low boil, then reduce the heat to low and cover the pan. Cook, stirring often, until the mixture is dense and ivory colored, about 2 hours. Stir in the candied citron, transfer to a large bowl, and refrigerate until cold. You can do this the day before, if you like.

Preheat the oven to 350°F (180°C). Spread the almonds on a baking sheet and toast them until light golden and fragrant. Let cool completely, then grind in a mini food processor until they resemble coarse sand. Set aside.

Butter a 9-by-13-by-2-inch (23-by-33-by-5-centimeter) baking pan (it has to be large enough so that the rice can be spread to a depth of about 1 inch/2.5 centimeters) and sprinkle with bread crumbs to lightly coat the pan.

In a large bowl, whisk the eggs, almonds, and rum until well combined, then fold in the cold rice mixture. Spread the mixture in the prepared pan and bake for about 1 hour, until firm and golden. Immediately sprinkle the top with the liqueur. Let cool completely but do not refrigerate. You can cut the cake into any shapes you like. For the traditional presentation, cut the cake lengthwise into four 13-inch-long strips, then cut each strip on an angle to make 5 diamonds per strip. (You'll end up with a few little scrap triangles at the end, which you can eat immediately as your reward for all this baking.) Serve with toothpicks. It's best eaten immediately, but leftovers will keep a day or two.

Milk ✕ 4 cups (32 fluid ounces/ 960 milliliters)

Sugar ✕ 1¼ cups (8¾ ounces/250 grams)

Grated zest of ½ lemon

Salt ✕ ¼ teaspoon

White rice ✕ ½ cup (3½ ounces/100 grams)

Candied citron or candied lemon peel ✕ 2½ ounces/70 grams, finely minced

Whole almonds ✕ ½ cup (3 ounces/85 grams)

Butter for the pan

Plain bread crumbs for the pan

Eggs ✕ 9 large, beaten

Rum ✕ ½ cup (4 fluid ounces/120 milliliters)

Almond liqueur, such as Amaretto ✕ 4 tablespoons

chocolate "salami"

Salame al cioccolato

SERVES 4 TO 6

aver le fette di salame sugli occhi.

TO HAVE SLICES OF SALAMI OVER YOUR EYES.
(MISSING THE OBVIOUS.)

This is an adorable dessert. It really looks like a salami, especially the way Italians serve it: coated in confectioners' sugar, tied with kitchen twine like real salami, and placed on a wooden cutting board. When it's sliced, the nuts and cookie bits add to the salami look on the inside, too.

Put the chocolate in a small bowl and melt it, either in a microwave oven or over a saucepan of gently simmering water. Let cool to room temperature and set aside.

Beat the butter with a whisk or electric mixer until creamy and smooth. Stir in the chocolate, cookies, nuts, and espresso until well combined. Spoon the mixture onto a sheet of plastic wrap or parchment paper and form into a salami shape about 6 inches (15 centimeters) long and 2 inches (5 centimeters) thick. Wrap well and refrigerate until firm, about 4 hours.

To serve, roll the "salami" in confectioners' sugar and tie with kitchen twine so it looks even more like the real thing.

Dark chocolate ✖ 2 ounces/55 grams

Butter ✖ 5 tablespoons (2½ ounces/ 70 grams), softened

Butter cookies, such as petit buerre ✖ 8 ounces/226 grams, coarsely chopped

Nuts, such as pistachios or hazelnuts, coarsely chopped ✖ 4 heaping tablespoons

Brewed espresso, or rum ✖ 1 tablespoon

Confectioners' sugar

CHAPTER TWO

cakes and sweet breads

TORTE E PANE DOLCE

the ultimate moist and tender chocolate cake

Torta tenerina

SERVES 8

REGION: Emilia-Romagna

This flourless cake, which has a crisp, macaroon-like outer layer and a dense, incredibly moist center, is by far one of the best tasting chocolate desserts I've ever tried. As the cake cools, it collapses just a little, creating a pretty webbing on the delicious crust.

It's made with only five ingredients, so be sure to use only top-quality chocolate, as it really stands out. This is a must-try recipe.

Preheat the oven to 350°F (180°C). Butter a 9-inch (23-centimeter) springform cake pan (see Note).

Put the chocolate and butter in a small bowl and melt them, either in a microwave oven or over a saucepan of gently simmering water.

In a large bowl, beat the granulated sugar and egg yolks with an electric mixer until creamy and pale yellow. Add the chocolate mixture and beat until creamy. Add the potato starch and mix until well combined.

In a separate large bowl, using clean, dry beaters, beat the egg whites until stiff. Slowly, using a clean spatula, fold the egg whites, a little at a time, into the chocolate mixture until combined. Spread the batter evenly into the prepared pan. Bake for about 20 minutes, until just set and firm in the center. Do not overbake: The cake will continue to set as it cools. Cool on a wire rack for about 30 minutes (the top will collapse and the crust will crack a bit) before cutting. Serve warm or at room temperature.

NOTE: You can also make this cake in a slightly larger or smaller springform pan, or in a square or rectangular pan, or even in individual-serving ramekins. Just adjust the cooking time accordingly.

Butter ✕ 7 tablespoons (3½ ounces/100 grams)

Dark chocolate ✕ 7 ounces/200 grams

Sugar ✕ 1 cup (7 ounces/200 grams)

Eggs ✕ 4 large, separated

Potato starch or cornstarch ✕ 2 tablespoons

il tenero rompe il duro.

TENDER TRUMPS TOUGH.

7 cups cake

Torta dei 7 vasetti

SERVES 10 TO 12

REGION: Throughout Italy

tutto fa brodo.
EVERYTHING MAKES SOUP.

Almost every Italian knows this recipe by heart. Embarrassingly simple to make, the cake's name comes from the fact that the ingredients equal seven "cups," using a yogurt container as the cup measure.

I love how the yogurt and olive oil combine to create a wonderful clean tart-sweet taste. It's great plain or served with a dollop of homemade jam.

Plain yogurt (see Note) ✳ 1 container
(6-fluid ounce/180-milliliter)

Olive or other vegetable oil ✳ 1 container

Sugar ✳ 2 containers

00 flour ✳ 3 containers

Eggs ✳ 3 large

Baking powder ✳ 2 teaspoons

UN ALTRO MODO

Apple Rosemary Cake: Add 1 to 2 peeled and diced apples and 2 tablespoons minced fresh rosemary.

Chocolate Cake: Add 2 tablespoons unsweetened cocoa powder and 2 ounces/55 grams chopped dark chocolate.

Spice Cake: Add 2 handfuls of chopped panforte or panpepato, Italy's famed spiced fruit and nut cake, available online or in gourmet shops.

Sublime Citrus Cake: Add grated orange, lime, or lemon zest.

Peach Cake: Add 1 to 2 diced fresh peaches.

Preheat the oven to 350°F (180°C). Lightly oil a standard 12-cup (2480-milliliter) tube cake pan and dust with flour.

Empty the container of yogurt into a bowl and, using the empty container as a measure, add the oil, sugar, and flour. Add the eggs and baking powder. Using an electric mixer, blend the ingredients until well combined and free of lumps. The dough will be fairly dense. If you like, you can add flavorings (see Un Altro Modo, left, for suggestions). Pour into the prepared pan and bake for about 45 minutes, until a toothpick inserted in the center comes out clean. Let cool on a rack before turning out of the pan. Serve warm or at room temperature.

NOTE: Since the yogurt container determines the proportions of the other ingredients, you can use a slightly smaller or larger container of yogurt, depending on how big a cake you'd like. I've tested the recipe with 4- and 8-fluid-ounce (120-milliliter and 240-milliliter) containers, as well as the 6-fluid-ounce/180-milliliter container described. The cake came out perfect in all cases, but with the larger containers, it needed a little more time in the oven.

torta paradiso

SERVES 8 TO 10

REGION: Lombardy, but popular throughout northern Italy

This tangy, moist lemon cake with a terrific crunchy crust has an incredibly silky mouthfeel. Described by many Italians as *la torta dei ricordi,* it's a "memory-lane" cake that their mothers had waiting for them on the kitchen table after school. Aptly named, it's heavenly tasting.

soli non si starebbe bene nemmeno in paradiso.
ONE CAN'T BE HAPPY ALONE, EVEN IN PARADISE.

Preheat the oven to 350°F. Butter and flour a 9½-inch (23.75-centimeter) round cake pan.

In a medium bowl, using an electric mixer, beat the egg yolks with 1 cup (7 ounces/200 grams) of the sugar until fluffy and light yellow. Set aside.

In a large bowl, using an electric mixer, beat the butter with the remaining ⅔ cup (6½ ounces/180 grams) sugar until fluffy. Beat in the egg-yolk mixture, flour, potato starch, baking powder, lemon zest, and lemon juice until well combined. Set the batter aside.

In a medium bowl, using clean, dry beaters, beat the egg whites until stiff peaks form. Fold the whites, a little at a time, into the batter until combined. Pour the batter into the prepared pan.

Bake for about 50 minutes, or until a toothpick inserted in the center comes out clean. Cool to room temperature in the pan on a wire rack, then turn the cake out of the pan.

Sprinkle with confectioners' sugar and serve. It's best eaten within a day or two.

Butter ✕ 12 tablespoons (6 ounces/ 170 grams)

00 flour ✕ ⅔ cup (3 ounces/85 grams), sifted

Egg yolks ✕ 6 large

Sugar ✕ 1⅔ cups (11½ ounces/330 grams)

Potato starch ✕ 1¼ cups (5 ounces/ 140 grams), sifted

Baking powder ✕ 2 teaspoons

Grated zest and juice of 1 lemon

Egg whites ✕ 2 large

Confectioners' sugar

capri's flourless chocolate-almond cake

Torta caprese

SERVES 10

REGION: Campania

*chi capri non vede,
paradiso non crede.*
IF YOU HAVEN'T SEEN CAPRI,
YOU CAN'T BELIEVE IN HEAVEN.

Dark chocolate and finely ground almonds meld into a densely rich flourless cake, with a crisp top crust and moist center. This traditional Italian dessert, created on the island of Capri, is one of Italy's most popular desserts. Since *torta caprese* is such a classic, I felt it was my duty to taste-test at least a dozen examples during a recent visit to Italy! Chef Mimmo di Raffaele, of the famed Hotel Caruso in Ravello, prepared my absolute favorite. He adds lemon zest to the traditional recipe, and that teeny hint of citrus really makes the chocolate flavor pop.

Butter ✳ 10 tablespoons (5 ounces/ 140 grams)

Cornstarch or potato flour for the pan

Whole blanched almonds ✳ 1 cup (5 ounces/140 grams)

Dark chocolate ✳ 5 ounces/140 grams, chopped

Sugar ✳ ¾ cup plus 1 tablespoon (5¾ ounces/165 grams)

Unsweetened cocoa powder ✳ 1½ tablespoons

Eggs ✳ 3 large, separated

Grated zest of 1 lemon

Pure vanilla extract ✳ 1 tablespoon

Confectioners' sugar

Preheat the oven to 350°F (180°C). Butter a 9-inch (23-centimeter) round cake pan and lightly dust with cornstarch.

Spread the almonds on a baking sheet and toast until lightly golden. Let cool to room temperature, then grind in a food processor until the texture resembles coarse sand. The almonds should not be ground too fine. Set aside.

Put the chocolate in a small bowl and melt it, either in a microwave oven or over a saucepan of gently simmering water, then add the butter and stir until melted and combined. Let cool slightly.

Using an electric mixer, beat together the egg yolks and sugar until creamy and light yellow. In a steady stream, add the chocolate-butter mixture and beat until combined. Beat in the ground almonds, lemon zest, and vanilla until combined.

In a separate bowl, beat the egg whites until stiff peaks form. Gently, a little at a time, using a wooden spoon or spatula, fold the chocolate mixture into the egg whites. Spread the batter in the prepared pan and bake for about 40 minutes, until a toothpick inserted in the center comes out clean. The surface will be cracked; this is normal. Cool completely in the pan on a wire rack, then turn the cake out of the pan. Sprinkle with confectioners' sugar and serve.

NOTE: This flourless cake is ideal for those with wheat allergies!

luscious olive oil–lemon cake

Caprese al limone

SERVES 10

REGION: Campania

This is a galaxy far, far away from any lemon cake you've ever tasted! The olive oil not only makes for an insanely moist cake, but it really brings out the flavor of the lemon, creating a lovely citrus tang.

Caprese, which means "from Capri," is a dark chocolate and almond cake first created on the island of Capri off the Amalfi coast. A popular variation, made instead with white chocolate and lemons, is called *caprese al limone*. Salvatore De Riso, one of Italy's most renowned pastry chefs, makes this variation, which uses olive oil instead of butter. He also adds a bit of candied lemon peel, a great trick that adds loads of flavor and moisture.

Preheat the oven to 375°F (190°C). Lightly oil a 9-inch (23-centimeter) round cake pan and dust with potato starch.

In a food processor, grind the almonds and confectioners' sugar until the mixture resembles fine sand. Add the vanilla, white chocolate, candied lemon peel, lemon zest, potato starch, baking powder, and baking soda and process until well combined. Add the oil and process until combined. Set aside.

With an electric mixer, beat the eggs and granulated sugar until they triple in volume, at least 10 minutes. Using a spatula or wooden spoon, slowly incorporate the almond mixture into the egg-sugar mixture until combined. The eggs will deflate a little; that's normal.

Pour the batter into the prepared pan and bake for 5 minutes, then lower the oven temperature to 320°F (160°C) and bake for about 40 minutes, until a toothpick inserted in the center comes out clean. Cool in the pan on a wire rack for at least 1 hour, then turn the cake out of the pan and let cool to room temperature.

Sprinkle with confectioners' sugar and serve.

Extra-virgin olive oil ✳ 6 tablespoons

Potato starch or cornstarch ✳ ¼ cup (1 ounces/30 grams)

Whole almonds ✳ 1¼ cups (7 ounces/ 200 grams)

Confectioners' sugar ✳ 1 cup (3½ ounces/100 grams)

Pure vanilla extract ✳ 2 teaspoons

White chocolate ✳ 6 ounces/170 grams, grated on a cheese grater

Candied lemon peel ✳ 3 heaping tablespoons

Grated zest of 3 lemons

Baking powder ✳ 2 teaspoons

Baking soda ✳ ½ teaspoon

Eggs ✳ 5 large

Sugar ✳ 4 tablespoons

rustic tuscan apple cake

Torta di mele

SERVES 8 TO 10

REGION: Tuscany

A classic! At first glance it may seem like a huge ratio of apple to dough and you're going to be tempted to cut down on the apples. Don't! They magically meld into the batter, and you'll love the result. The top half of the *torta* is chock full of tender apples that float over sweet, moist cake. This is a deceptively simple recipe that yields exceptional results.

Butter ✳ 2 tablespoons

00 flour ✳ 1¾ cups (7 ounces/200 grams)

Sugar ✳ ⅔ cup plus 1 tablespoon (5 ounces/140 grams)

Eggs ✳ 2 large

Milk ✳ ½ cup (4 fluid ounces/120 milliliters)

Baking powder ✳ 2 teaspoons

Baking soda ✳ 1 teaspoon

Grated zest of 1 lemon

Apples ✳ 4 small (about 2 pounds/910 grams)

Preheat the oven to 350°F (180°C). Butter and flour an 8-inch (20-centimeter) round cake pan.

In a large bowl, using a whisk or an electric mixer, beat the ⅔ cup (4½ ounces/130 grams) sugar and the eggs until creamy and light yellow. Beat in the flour, milk, baking powder, baking soda, and lemon zest. Pour the batter into the prepared pan.

Peel and core the apples. Dice one and sprinkle it over the batter. Cut the remaining apples into thin slices and spread them in a neat pattern over the diced apples in the pan. Scatter thin pats of butter over the apples and sprinkle with the remaining 1 tablespoon sugar. Bake for about 75 minutes, until dark golden and a toothpick inserted in the center comes out clean.

in italy

Practically everyone in Italy knows Disney's Elvira "Grandma Duck" Coot, Donald Duck's grandmother. *Nonna Papera,* as she's known, is spry, has all sorts of adventures, and yet bakes up beautiful pies. She was so popular in Italy that a children's cookbook called *Manuale di Nonna Papera* was published in 1970. It became a phenomenal success and is the source of many fond foodie memories for millions of Italians. To compliment a particularly lovely cake Italians will often say, *"Pareva la torta di Nonna Papera!"* —it looks like Grandma Duck's cake!

salad bowl cake

Parrozzo

SERVES 4 TO 6

REGION: Abruzzo

I smile every time I think of this cake. It's really cute! Baked in a small metal salad bowl, it comes out as an adorable little dome, which is then covered in dark chocolate. Semolina flour, the essential ingredient for making authentic Italian pasta, gives this cake a pleasing grainy texture, while the almond flour adds lushness. Both almond and semolina flour are easily found in health food stores and even in many supermarkets in the United States.

Butter ✕ 4 tablespoons (2 ounces/55 grams), softened

Semolina flour ✕ ½ cup plus 1 tablespoon (3½ ounces/100 grams)

Eggs ✕ 4 large, separated

Sugar ✕ ¾ cup (5¼ ounces/150 grams)

Almond flour or very finely ground blanched almonds ✕ 1 cup (5 ounces/140 grams)

Grated zest and juice of ½ lemon

Pinch of salt

Dark chocolate ✕ 2½ ounces/70 grams, chopped

Preheat the oven to 320°F (155°C). Butter and flour a metal bowl about 3 cups– (720 milliliters–) size, that is 6 inches (15 centimeters) in diameter. Line the bottom of the bowl with a circle of parchment paper and butter and flour the paper.

In a large bowl, using an electric mixer, beat the egg yolks and sugar until fluffy and light yellow. Using a wooden spoon or spatula, gradually stir in the semolina and almond flours, lemon zest, lemon juice, butter, and salt until well combined. Set the batter aside.

In a separate large bowl, using clean, dry beaters, beat the egg whites until very stiff peaks form. Gently fold the egg whites into the batter and pour into the prepared bowl. Bake for about 50 minutes, or until golden and a toothpick inserted in the center comes out clean. Remove from the oven, turn out onto a wire rack, and cool completely.

Put the chocolate in a small bowl and melt it, either in a microwave oven or over a saucepan of gently simmering water. Spread the chocolate over the cooled cake and let the chocolate set before serving.

in italy

Parrozzo is a typical dessert of Abruzzo, a region on the east coast of Italy. Its name comes from a domed bread made by the local fisherman, *pane rozzo,* or coarse bread, made with cornmeal, olive oil, and other local ingredients. In 1900, a pastry chef from the Abruzzo town of Pescara, Luigi D'Amico, transformed the bread into a dessert by adding almonds, sugar, and eggs and then coating the whole thing in chocolate so that it looked like the dark, golden, oven-baked *pane rozzo.* It became a hit in the region and was further popularized by the Italian poet Gabriele D'Annunzio, a friend of the chef's, who not only suggested the cake's name but also wrote a poem in its honor.

buckwheat red currant jam cake

Torta di grano saraceno

SERVES 12

REGION: Trentino–Alto Adige

It's no wonder this is one of northern Italy's most popular desserts. The fabulously earthy buckwheat gets a rich nuttiness from the hazelnut flour and a tang from the jam filling. If you like buckwheat pancakes, you'll love this cake.

Preheat the oven to 350°F (180°C). Butter and flour a 10-inch (25-centimeter) round cake pan.

In a large bowl, using an electric mixer, beat the butter and sugar until fluffy and light yellow. Beat in the egg yolks, one at a time, until creamy and well combined. Add the grappa.

Sift together the buckwheat flour, hazelnut flour, baking powder, and baking soda, and add—gradually, ¼ cup (35 grams) at a time—into the mixture, beating to combine after each addition. Set the batter aside.

In a separate large bowl, with clean and dry beaters, beat the egg whites and salt until stiff peaks form. Fold the whites into the batter. Spread the batter in the prepared pan and bake for 20 minutes, then increase the oven temperature to 375°F (190°C) and bake for 35 to 40 minutes longer, or until a toothpick in the center comes out clean. Cool to room temperature in the pan on a wire rack, then turn the cake out of the pan.

Using a long serrated knife, split the cake in half horizontally and spread the bottom layer with a generous amount of jam. Cover with the top layer and serve with whipped cream, if you like.

NOTE: You can find hazelnut flour in most supermarkets, or simply grind blanched hazelnuts in a mini food processor until the texture resembles fine sand.

Butter ✖ 8 tablespoons (4 ounces/115 grams)

Buckwheat flour ✖ 1⅓ cups (8 ounces/ 225 grams)

Sugar ✖ 1⅔ cups (11½ ounces/330 grams)

Eggs ✖ 6 large, separated

Grappa ✖ 2 tablespoons (optional)

Hazelnut flour or finely ground hazelnuts ✖ ½ cup (2½ ounces/70 grams)

Baking powder ✖ 3 teaspoons

Baking soda ✖ 1 teaspoon

Salt ✖ ¼ teaspoon

Red currant or other berry jam ✖ 1½ cups (12 fluid ounces/360 milliliters)

Whipped cream, optional

almond-cornmeal crumble with spicy chocolate sauce

Sbrisolona

SERVES 10

REGION: Lombardy

la polenta è utile per quattro cose: serve da minestra, serve da pane, sazia, e scalda le mani.

POLENTA IS GOOD FOR FOUR THINGS: TO MAKE SOUP, TO MAKE BREAD, TO FILL YOU UP, AND TO WARM YOUR HANDS.

Sbrisolona, which means "crumbly," is rustic and grainy, with a homey taste—more of a giant cookie than a cake. In fact, in Italy this dessert is not cut like a cake but rather broken with the hands or with a wooden spoon at the table, with everyone taking bits and pieces. A typical dessert of Lombardy that's so tightly tied to that region and Italian culinary heritage that authorities there have applied for official *denominatzione di origine controllata* (DOC) status. The cake is fabulous plain, but the chocolate sauce complements it nicely, creating a very intriguing flavor combination.

FOR THE CAKE:

Butter (see Note) ✕ 16 tablespoons (8 ounces/225 grams)

Fine-ground cornmeal ✕ 1 cup (5 ounces/140 grams)

All-purpose flour ✕ 2 cups (9 ounces/255 grams)

Sugar ✕ 1 cup (7 ounces/200 grams)

Almonds (either slivered or a mix of finely and coarsely chopped whole almonds) ✕ 1½ cups (7 ounces/200 grams)

Egg yolks ✕ 2 large

Pure vanilla extract ✕ 1 tablespoon

Grated zest of 1 lemon

FOR THE CHOCOLATE SAUCE:

Dark chocolate ✕ 3½ ounces/100 grams, chopped

Heavy cream ✕ ½ cup (4 fluid ounces/120 milliliters)

Pinch of hot red pepper flakes

Almond liqueur, such as Amaretto ✕ 2 tablespoons

Make the cake: Preheat the oven to 350°F (180°C). Butter a 10- to 11-inch (25- to 28-centimeter) springform pan and dust with cornmeal.

In a large bowl, combine the butter, cornmeal, flour, sugar, almonds, egg yolks, vanilla, and lemon zest, crumbling the ingredients with your fingers until just coarsely combined. It should look lumpy and dry. Take loose handfuls of the mixture and sprinkle it into the prepared pan. It will be irregular and should be very crumbly and freeform. Do not press it smooth or compact it: It will come together as it bakes. Top with a scattering of almond slivers or whole almonds, if you like.

Bake for 50 to 60 minutes, until golden at the edges and a toothpick inserted in the center comes out clean. Cool to room temperature in the pan on a wire rack.

Make the chocolate sauce: Just before serving, put the chocolate and cream in a medium bowl and melt the chocolate, either in a microwave oven or over a saucepan of gently simmering water. Add red pepper flakes and liqueur, to taste.

Serve the cake at room temperature with the warm chocolate sauce on the side.

NOTE: If you'd like an even crisper cake, substitute lard for the butter.

bread crumb–chocolate cake

Torta di pane e cioccolato

SERVES 12

REGION: Emilia-Romagna, and throughout northern Italy

"A cup of bread crumbs and no sugar! You've got to be kidding," I exclaimed when a Bologna pastry chef, Olimpia Apogeo, e-mailed me this recipe. It took two phone calls, several more e-mails, and a Skype session to finally convince me to try it. I remained skeptical even as it went into the oven. But what came out was fantastic! Rustic, with a pleasingly grainy texture, the bread crumbs turned out to be a wonderful canvas for dark chocolate. Just like bread and chocolate, but as cake.

Made entirely in a food processor, this cake takes only minutes to prepare. I especially like the hint of bitter almonds from the *amaretti* cookies, which nicely highlights the chocolate.

Butter and flour for the pan

Crisp *amaretti* (almond cookies) ✳ 54 cookies (about 7 ounces/200 grams)

Plain bread crumbs ✳ 1⅓ cups (7 ounces/200 grams)

Dark chocolate ✳ 7 ounces/198 grams, chopped

Heavy cream ✳ 1½ cups (12 fluid ounces/360 milliliters)

Eggs ✳ 3 large

Rum, or liqueur such as Sassolino ✳ 4 tablespoons

Baking powder ✳ 1½ tablespoons

Confectioners' sugar

Preheat the oven to 350°F (180°C). Butter and lightly flour a 9-inch (23-centimeter) round cake pan.

Grind the cookies in a food processor until the texture resembles coarse sand.

Add the bread crumbs and chocolate and process until the chocolate is finely chopped and the mixture resembles coarse sand. Add the cream, eggs, rum, and baking powder and process until well combined. The dough will be very thick and dense. Spread the dough evenly in the prepared pan and bake for about 35 minutes, until the center is firm to the touch. Do not overbake. Cool to room temperature on a wire rack, then turn the cake out of the pan.

Sprinkle with confectioners' sugar and serve.

UN ALTRO MODO

Double Bread Crumb: Instead of the *amaretti* cookies, add another 1 cup (8 ounces/190 grams) bread crumbs and honey to taste.

Any-Cookie Bread Crumb Cake: Substitute another type of cookie—like *cantucci* or *savoiardi*—for the *amaretti*.

Bread and Jam Cake: Ice the cake with jam or swirl ½ cup (4 ounces/100 grams) jam into the batter.

Anything-Goes Bread Crumb Cake: Add ½ cup (2 ounces/55 grams) crushed nuts or ½ cup (4 fluid ounces/120 milliliters) fresh fruit to the batter.

rum babà cake

SERVES 10

REGION: Campania, especially Naples, but now found throughout Italy

sì nu babà.

YOU ARE A BABÀ. (NEAPOLITAN
FOR A PARTICULARLY
NICE PERSON.)

A moist, yeasty, briochelike cake saturated with sweet rum syrup, this is one of my favorite desserts. It not only is easy to make and stays moist for days, but the homemade cake tastes just as good as pastry-shop versions. In Naples, babà are sold individually in their traditional mushroom shape, and also in larger cake-sized portions. Babà are eaten either plain or with pastry cream or whipped cream, and topped with fresh fruit like tiny wild strawberries.

In a large bowl, combine the yeast, milk, and ¼ cup (1¾ ounces/ 50 grams) of the sugar and let rest for about 3 minutes, until it bubbles. Using an electric mixer, beat in the eggs, egg yolk, and butter until smooth. Gradually mix in the flour, a little at a time, until combined. Stir in the orange zest and salt. Let rest, lightly covered with plastic wrap, until the dough doubles, about 45 minutes.

Preheat the oven to 375°F (190°C). Butter and flour a nonstick standard 12-cup tube cake pan.

In a medium saucepan, bring 1½ cup (12 fluid ounces/360 milliliters) water and the remaining 3 cups (21 ounces/600 grams) sugar to a boil. Lower the heat and simmer until thickened, stirring occasionally, about 20 minutes. Remove from the heat, stir in the lemon zest, and set aside.

Meanwhile press the dough into the prepared pan and set aside to rise a second time, about 20 minutes. Bake until golden, about 20 minutes. Let the cake cool just enough to turn it out of the pan and transfer it to a serving platter.

One hour before serving the cake, add the rum, to taste, to the sugar syrup, and slowly, in drops, pour the rum syrup over the cake until it is completely absorbed. Serve at room temperature.

Active dry yeast ⊗ 4½ teaspoons (2 envelopes)

Milk ⊗ ½ cup (4 fluid ounces/120 milliliters), warmed

Sugar ⊗ 3 cups plus ¼ cup (22¾ ounces/ 650 grams)

Eggs ⊗ 3 large

Egg yolk ⊗ 1 large

Butter ⊗ 8 tablespoons (4 ounces/ 115 grams), melted

All-purpose flour ⊗ 2 cups (9 ounces/ 255 grams)

Grated zest of ½ orange

Salt ⊗ ¼ teaspoon

Grated zest of 1 lemon

Dark rum ⊗ ¼ to ¾ cup (2 to 6 fluid ounces/60 to 180 milliliters)

cornmeal-apple good luck cake

Pinza

SERVES 10

REGION: Veneto and Friuli–Venezia Giulia

This is a moist, orange-scented yeast cake bursting with apples, dried fruit, and nuts. Eating *pinza* during the New Year celebrations is supposed to bring good luck, and many Italians will even wrap a slice in a white linen napkin and save it for months to hold on to the promise of good fortune.

One of my favorite legends surrounding pinza is that if a woman wants to be married within the year, all she needs to do is eat seven slices in seven different homes she visits on January 6 for the Feast of the Epiphany.

Milk ✂ 2 cups (16 fluid ounces/
480 milliliters)

Grated zest of ½ lemon

Honey ✂ 1 tablespoon

Corn, or other vegetable oil ✂ 7 tablespoons

Fine-ground cornmeal ✂ ½ cup
(2½ ounces/70 grams)

Active dry yeast ✂ 2¼ teaspoons
(1 envelope)

Raisins ✂ 1 cup (5 ounces/140 grams)

Dried figs ✂ 10 to 12, thinly sliced

Chopped walnuts ✂ 2 tablespoons

Pine nuts ✂ 1 tablespoon

Fennel seeds ✂ 1 teaspoon

Sugar ✂ 5 tablespoons

Salt ✂ 1 teaspoon

All-purpose flour ✂ 3 cups (13½ ounces/
385 grams)

In a medium saucepan, bring ¾ cup (6 fluid ounces/180 milliliters) of the milk, the lemon zest, honey, and 1 tablespoon of the oil to a boil. Gradually sprinkle in the cornmeal and cook, stirring to remove any lumps, until the mixture thickens to a dense paste, about 2 minutes. Remove from the heat and let cool to room temperature.

Warm the remaining milk and pour it into a large bowl. Sprinkle the yeast over the milk, allow it to bubble, and stir to dissolve. Add the raisins, figs, walnuts, pine nuts, fennel, 1 tablespoon of the granulated sugar, the salt, 1 tablespoon of the oil, and ½ cup (2 ounces/55 grams) of the flour and stir until well combined. Cover with plastic wrap and let rest for 15 minutes.

Preheat the oven to 350°F (180°C) and line the bottom and sides of a rectangular baking pan, roughly 10 by 12 inches (30.5 by 25 centimeters), with parchment paper.

Add the remaining 6 tablespoons oil, the butter, and the cornmeal mixture to the yeast mixture and stir well to remove any lumps. Add the apple slices, pumpkin, orange zest, and remaining 4 tablespoons granulated sugar and mix until well combined.

Gradually add the remaining 2½ cups (11¼ ounces/315 grams) flour, combining thoroughly after each addition.

Spread the mixture in the prepared pan, cover loosely with aluminum foil, and bake for 15 minutes. Remove the foil and continue baking for 15 to 20 minutes longer, until golden. Cool to room temperature on a wire rack. Sprinkle with confectioners' sugar and serve. The cake will stay fresh for two to three days.

Butter ✳ 10 tablespoons (5 ounces/140 grams), melted

One small firm apple, peeled and thinly sliced

Mashed cooked pumpkin, or canned, unsweetened pumpkin puree ✳ 4 heaping tablespoons

Grated zest of ½ orange

Confectioners' sugar

intensely chocolate italian lava cakes

peccati di gola.
SINS OF THE THROAT.

SERVES 6

REGION: Piedmont, and throughout northern Italy

Just five ingredients and ten minutes to chocolate bliss, this is a foolproof recipe. Dessert doesn't get much better than this—oozy, rich, fudgy, chocolate in the center and a dense, moist cake around it. This recipe, given to me by G. B. Martelli of Venchi chocolates, is one you must try to appreciate just how luscious fine Italian chocolate is.

Preheat the oven to 400°F (200°C). Butter six ½-cup (4-fluid ounce/120-milliliter) ramekins.

In a large bowl, with an electric mixer, beat the eggs and sugar together until smooth. Add the flour and beat to combine.

Put the chocolate and butter in a small bowl and melt them, either in a microwave oven or over a saucepan of gently simmering water. Beat the chocolate mixture into the egg mixture.

Divide the batter among the prepared ramekins. Put the ramekins on a baking sheet and bake for about 10 minutes, until set. Turn each ramekin upside down onto a serving plate and unmold. Serve warm.

Butter ✳ 8 tablespoons (4 ounces/115 grams)

Eggs ✳ 3 large

Sugar ✳ ½ cup (3½ ounces/100 grams)

All-purpose flour ✳ ¼ cup (1 ounces/30 grams)

Dark chocolate (preferably Venchi brand) ✳ 6 ounces/170 grams

sweet rosemary and grape focaccia

Schiacciata all'uva

SERVES 6.

REGION: Tuscany

This dessert is actually two focaccias, one baked right over the other, stuffed and topped with plump grapes. The bottom crust bakes thin and crisp, while the top puffs up tender and cakey. Some of the grapes collapse a little and release pools of pretty purple juice, while others stay whole. When you take a bite, you get the satisfying chewiness of bread, crunchy in spots, plus the warm grapes, which burst in your mouth. It's sophisticated and rustic at the same time. *Schiacciata*—meaning "flattened or squashed"—is the term they use in Florence for foccacia.

Olive oil ✕ 10 tablespoons (5 fluid ounces/150 milliliters)

Fresh rosemary, finely minced ✕ 2 tablespoons

Active dry yeast ✕ 2¼ teaspoons (1 envelope)

Warm water ✕ ½ cup

All-purpose flour ✕ 2 cups (10½ ounces/ 297 grams)

Sugar ✕ 11 tablespoons (4½ ounces/ 130 grams)

Salt ✕ ½ teaspoon

Black seedless grapes ✕ 3 pounds (1.4 kilograms), stems removed

Anise seeds ✕ 2 teaspoons

In a small saucepan, heat 4 tablespoons of the oil and the rosemary until warm. Set aside to cool to room temperature.

Sprinkle the yeast into the warm water and set it aside until it bubbles, about 2 minutes. Sift the flour onto a work surface or into a large bowl. Make a well in the center and fill with the yeast water, the rosemary oil, 3 table-spoons of the sugar, and the salt. Gradually incorporate the flour into the liquid in the well until a dough forms. Knead the dough until smooth, then set it aside in a lightly oiled bowl until it doubles, about 1 hour.

Preheat the oven to 350°F (180°C). Coat a 9-by-13-inch (23-by-33-centimeter) baking pan with 2 tablespoons of the oil.

Put about half of the grapes into a bowl and, using a large fork or potato masher, gently break the skins. Stir in the remaining grapes whole.

Take slightly more than half of the dough and roll it out to fit the baking pan. Put the dough into the prepared pan and brush with 2 tablespoons of the oil. Top with a little more than half of the crushed and whole grapes. Sprinkle with 4 tablespoons of the sugar and 1 teaspoon of the anise.

Roll out and stretch the remaining dough to fit the pan. It will be thin. Place the dough over the grape layer. It's okay if it doesn't fully cover the bottom layer. Spread with the remaining 2 tablespoons oil, and the remaining grapes, 4 tablespoons sugar, and 1 teaspoon anise. Bake for about 1 hour, until the top is golden brown. Serve at room temperature.

lemon brioche "rose" cake

Torta di rose

SERVES 9

REGION: Emilia-Romagna

This has been a popular dessert in Italy since the Renaissance, when it was often served at wedding feasts. Appropriate, since it looks like a lovely bouquet of roses! Today in Italy, especially the north, it's a favorite mid-morning or afternoon snack. It's sort of like a cluster of cinnamon buns, but lemon-flavored.

Milk ✖ ¾ cup (6 fluid ounces/180 milliliters)

Active dry yeast ✖ 2¼ teaspoons (1 envelope)

All-purpose flour ✖ 2½ cups (11¼ ounces/315 grams)

Egg yolks ✖ 2 large

Sugar ✖ ⅔ cup plus ¼ cup (6¼ ounces/ 180 grams)

Olive oil ✖ 2 tablespoons

Salt ✖ ¼ teaspoon

Butter ✖ 8 tablespoons (4 ounces/115 grams)

Grated zest of 1 lemon

Ground cinnamon ✖ ½ teaspoon

Egg white ✖ 1 large, lightly beaten

Confectioners' sugar

Warm ¼ cup (2 fluid ounces/60 milliliters) of the milk into a large bowl. Sprinkle the yeast over the milk, allow it to bubble, and stir to dissolve. Sift in ½ cup (2 ounces/55 grams) of the flour and stir to combine, adding extra milk, a drop at a time, as needed until a dough forms. Knead the dough, right in the bowl, until smooth, cover with plastic wrap, and let rise in a warm place for at least 1 hour or overnight. This is the "starter."

To the starter, sift in the remaining 2 cups (9 ounces/255 grams) flour, then add the remaining ½ cup (4 fluid ounces/120 milliliters) milk, the egg yolks, 2 tablespoons of the granulated sugar, the oil, and salt. Stir until a dough forms, adding drops of extra milk as needed if the dough is too dry. Knead until smooth, then set the dough aside while you prepare the filling.

Lightly butter and flour a 9-inch (23-centimeter) round cake pan. In a medium bowl, with an electric mixer, beat together the butter, ⅔ cup (4½ ounces/130 grams) of the granulated sugar, the lemon zest, and cinnamon until smooth and creamy. Set aside.

Sprinkle a work surface with flour and roll the dough out into a rectangle about 12 by 18 inches (46 by 30.5 centimeters), and ½ inch (12 millimeters) thick. Spread the filling over the rectangle of dough, all the way to the edges, leaving a 1-inch (24-millimeter) strip uncovered at the long end farthest from you. Gently roll the dough, starting at the long end of the rectangle closest to you, up over itself, forming a spiral. Using a sharp knife, cut nine 1½-inch-(36-millimeter) thick slices of the roll. Arrange the slices, cut side down, in the prepared pan. Cover with plastic wrap and let rise for 1 hour. Poke the dough to test it. If the indentation stays, it's ready to bake.

Preheat the oven to 350°F (180°C). Brush the cake with the egg white and sprinkle with the remaining 2 tablespoons granulated sugar. Bake for about 35 minutes, until golden. Cool to room temperature in the pan. Sprinkle with confectioners' sugar. To serve, have your guests pull off a "rose," and eat it out of hand.

cantaloupe cake

Torta di melone

SERVES 12

REGION: Piedmont

gli uomini sono come i meloni: molti cattivi e pochi buoni.

MEN ARE LIKE MELONS: LOTS OF BAD ONES AND ONLY A FEW GOOD ONES.

Speckled with pretty orange bits of cantaloupe, this cake is as lovely as it is luscious. Cantaloupe adds an amazing moistness and natural sweetness to this outstanding quick-to-assemble cake. The hint of Asti Spumante provides its enticing aroma.

Diced cantaloupe ⁙ 3 cups (17 ounces/480 grams)

Asti Spumante ⁙ 2 cups (16 fluid ounces/ 480 milliliters)

Butter for the pan

All-purpose flour ⁙ 2 cups (8 ounces/ 225 grams)

Eggs ⁙ 2 large, separated

Sugar ⁙ 1 cup plus 2 tablespoons (8 ounces/225 grams)

Baking powder ⁙ 2 teaspoons

Combine the melon and wine in a bowl and let rest for at least 30 minutes to infuse the melon with the wine's flavors.

Preheat the oven to 360°F (180°C). Lightly butter and flour a standard 12-cup Bundt pan.

In a large bowl, using an electric mixer or whisk, beat together the egg yolks and sugar until creamy and light yellow. Gradually, adding a little at a time, beat in the flour and baking powder until combined. Set the batter aside.

In a medium bowl, with clean and dry beaters, beat the egg whites until stiff peaks form. Fold the whites into the batter until combined. Using a slotted spoon, add the cantaloupe and about 2 tablespoons of the liquid to the batter and stir until just combined. Spread the batter evenly in the prepared pan and bake for about 50 minutes, until golden and a toothpick inserted into the center comes out clean. Serve at room temperature.

fig and rosemary honey focaccia

Focaccia di fichi e rosmarino

SERVES 6 TO 8

REGION: Tuscany

Take advantage of fig season with this fragrant and unusual dessert. It's sweet, but not too sweet, with a satisfying mix of crunchy and chewy textures.

al fico l'acqua, alla pesca il vino.

GIVE FIGS WATER, PEACHES WINE. (IN ITALY, FIGS ARE GENERALLY SERVED IN A BOWL OF WATER TO COOL THEM, WHILE PEACHES ARE OFTEN SERVED SLICED IN A GLASS OF WINE.)

Sprinkle the yeast over the warm water and let the yeast bubble, about 2 minutes. Sift the flour onto a work surface or into a large bowl. Make a well in the center and fill with the yeast water, oil, sugar, and salt. Gradually incorporate the flour into the liquid, until a dough forms. Add a few drops more water if needed. Knead the dough until smooth, then set aside in a lightly oiled bowl until it doubles, about 1 hour.

Preheat the oven to 350°F (180°C). Oil a 10-inch (25-centimeter) round springform cake pan.

Using your hands, press the dough out into the prepared pan. Pierce the dough all over with a fork.

Carefully cut a cross into the bottom of one of the figs, halfway down, so the fig opens like a flower. Press it into the center of the dough. Slice the remaining figs in half and arrange them around the center fig, cut side up, pressing them into the dough as far as possible.

Put the honey, rosemary, and lemon juice in a small bowl and stir until well combined. Using a pastry brush, spread the mixture over the top of the figs and dough. Bake for about 25 minutes, until golden and cooked through. Remove from the oven and drizzle with more honey and sprigs of rosemary. Serve warm.

NOTE: You can also substitute dried figs that have been rehydrated by simmering them for 15 minutes in 1 cup (8 ounces/240 milliliters) of white wine or white grape juice.

Active dry yeast ✳ 2¼ teaspoons (1 envelope)

Warm water ✳ ½ cup (4 fluid ounces/ 120 milliliters)

All-purpose flour ✳ 2 cups (10½ ounces/ 298 grams)

Olive oil ✳ 2 tablespoons

Sugar ✳ 2 tablespoons

Salt ✳ ½ teaspoon

Fresh figs ✳ 16 to 18, stems removed

Honey ✳ 3 tablespoons

Fresh rosemary leaves ✳ 1 tablespoon

Juice of ½ lemon

pizza con nutella

MAKES 2 PIZZAS; EACH SERVES 6

REGION: Throughout Italy

*facendo scendere
la farina.*
TO SIFT FLOUR.
(TO ANALYZE.)

One day in Rome while researching this book, I got the idea to interview a hundred random Italians. I wanted a man-in-the-street sort of viewpoint on Italian sweets. So, with clipboard in hand, I stood in front of a bread shop popular with the locals and asked each person in line for their ten favorite Italian desserts. After the predictable favorites like *cantucci, panettone,* and *tiramisù,* I'd hear, almost apologetically, "*pizza bianca con Nutella*"—plain baked pizza dough smeared with the popular chocolate-hazelnut spread.

You can buy frozen readymade pizza dough in the supermarket or even from your local pizza shop, but I hope you'll try this terrific pizza dough recipe given to me by Margherita and Valeria Simili, identical septuagenarian twins, affectionately nicknamed *Sorelli Simili,* "similar sisters," with a play on the meaning of their last name.

Follow their simple directions, and you'll get a pizza crust that's chewy and crisp, never leathery. This recipe makes two pizzas. Don't need two dessert pizzas? After the dough has risen, freeze half. It keeps nicely for several weeks. Or cook one as a savory dinner pizza, topped with your favorite fixings. Dinner and dessert with one recipe. Sweet.

Bread flour (see Note) ✹ 3½ cups
(17 ounces/480 grams)

Active dry yeast ✹ 2¼ teaspoons
(1 envelope)

Room temperature bottled spring or filtered water ✹ 1 cup (8 fluid ounces/
240 milliliters)

Olive oil ✹ 4 tablespoons

Salt ✹ 1½ teaspoons

Semolina flour or coarse-ground cornmeal for the pans

Nutella or other *crema gianduia* spread

On a work surface or in a very large bowl, put the bread flour in a pile and make a well in the center. Put the yeast and ½ cup (4 fluid ounces/120 milliliters) of the water in the center of the well; stir and let rest until the yeast bubbles, about 3 minutes. Incorporate a little of the flour into the liquid to form a paste. Add the oil and salt and, taking a little flour at a time, gradually incorporate the flour and remaining water, until you've incorporated all the water. You might have a little flour left over; leave it on the side. Knead the dough until it is smooth and elastic, 5 to 8 minutes. Roll into a ball, put into a lightly oiled deep bowl, cover with plastic wrap, and let rest for 1½ hours.

Meanwhile, lightly dust two flat baking sheets or two flat baking pans about 12 by 16 inches (30.5 by 40.5 centimeters) with semolina flour.

Preheat the oven to 500°F (260°C) and set two racks in the lower third of the oven. (If you have a pizza stone or pizza baking tiles, preheat them in the lower third of the oven. But no worries if you don't have special equipment.)

Divide the dough in half. Roll each portion into a ball. Cover one ball with a damp cotton dishcloth as you work with the other ball.

Put the dough on a lightly floured surface, preferably a large wooden cutting board. The idea is to shape the ball into a thin round by pressing from the center out with your palms and then your fingertips at first. Then, holding the dough in place in the center with your palm, gently stretch the sides out and press them down with your other palm until you have a large, ½-inch- (12-millimeter) thick disk. Put the dough on one of the prepared baking sheets, brush with oil, pierce it all over with a fork, and immediately put the pan in the oven (or slide the dough onto the pizza stone) so it can bake while you work on the second ball of dough. Bake for about 8 minutes, then turn the pan 180 degrees so the pizza cooks evenly and bake it for another 8 to 10 minutes or until golden brown and cooked through.

Repeat with the other dough ball.

Let the pizzas cool slightly, then spread generously with Nutella. Serve immediately.

NOTE: If you prefer a flatter, crisper crust, use cake flour.

nutella

Che mondo sarebbe senza Nutella?—"What would the world be like without Nutella?"—may be Italy's most famous ad slogan. Gigi Padovani, famed Italian journalist and author of several books, including one on Nutella, notes, "Italians go crazy for Nutella because it reminds them of their childhood. Still today in Italy, every mom and grandmother who serves it to their children and grandchildren can't help but recall that first time they themselves enjoyed it for breakfast."

Nutella, a creamy hazelnut and chocolate spread, is not only immensely popular in Italy, but is also one of the country's best-known exports, sold in seventy-five countries worldwide. The product as we know it today was launched in 1964, but its roots are older. It was invented in the 1940s as a reaction to chocolate shortages resulting from World War II.

Initially called *supercrema gianduia* but rechristened in 1964, Nutella was created in Piedmont by Pietro Ferrero, pastry chef and founder of the Ferrero company. Beginning with gianduia, the popular mixture of finely ground hazelnut butter and chocolate, he added yet more hazelnuts to create a super-soft spreadable version of the treat. It's been a staple ever since.

CHAPTER THREE

refrigerator cakes

TORTE FREDDE

torta mimosa

REGION: Emilia-Romagna and popular throughout northern Italy

This cake, which looks like a bouquet of mimosa flowers, is eaten on March 8 in celebration of International Women's Day—*Festa della Donna*—a sort of BFF day celebrating womanhood and female friendships. It is one of my top five favorites in this book! But like a good female friendship, this recipe takes effort. The cake is made from two basic recipes: sponge cake and pastry cream. Each is worth learning, as with them you can make myriad classic Italian desserts. This lovely cake is better if eaten a day or two after it's made. It keeps nicely for up to a week and freezes perfectly.

Prepare the cake: Cool the cakes to room temperature.

Trim the crusts on one of the cakes so there are no dark parts showing. Carefully slice the cake in half horizontally so you have two layers. Set them aside. Trim the top and side crusts of the second cake, leaving the bottom dark. Carefully slice the cake in half horizontally. Set aside the bottom layer. Slice the remaining layer into 1/4-inch-wide (6-millimeter-wide) strips, then cut the strips into cubes. Set the cubes aside.

Assemble the cake: Put the sugar and 1/2 cup (4 fluid ounces/ 120 milliliters) water in a small saucepan and bring to a boil. Remove from the heat and stir in the liqueur. Let cool to room temperature.

Put the bottom cake layer on a serving plate. Moisten with one third of the liqueur syrup, then spread with a little less than one third of the pastry cream. Repeat with the next 2 layers, then spread the remaining pastry cream on the sides of the cake. Press the cake cubes onto the top and sides of the cake. Loosely cover with plastic wrap and refrigerate until set, about 2 hours. Serve cold. Leftovers can be refrigerated for up to 5 days or frozen for at least 6 weeks.

FOR THE SPONGE CAKE:

1 recipe Italian Sponge Cake (page 199), made as 2 (9-inch) cakes

TO ASSEMBLE THE CAKE:

Sugar ✖ 4 tablespoons

Sweet citrus liqueur, such as Cointreau or limoncello ✖ 4 tablespoons

1 recipe Pastry Cream (page 197), chilled until very cold, at least 4 hours

mocha hazelnut tart

Torta fredda di nocciole

SERVES 8

REGION: Piedmont

Creamy chocolate, with a hint of coffee, floats over a layer of crunchy hazelnuts. Other than the heat needed to melt the chocolate, this is a totally no-cook dessert that's served icy cold right from the refrigerator. A huge hit with everyone who tastes it, this recipe from Torino's La Maggiorana cooking school is a must-try.

fare la figura del cioccolataio

TO ACT LIKE A CHOCOLATE MAKER. (AN EXPRESSION USED IN TURIN TO DESCRIBE THE NOUVEAU RICHE. IT DATES TO 1823, WHEN KING CARLO FELICE DI SAVOIA NOTICED A FINER COACH THAN HIS OWN PASS BY AND DISCOVERED IT WAS OWNED BY A LOCAL CHOCOLATIER. BACK THEN, CHOCOLATE WAS SO PRIZED THAT CHOCOLATIERS OFTEN BECAME QUITE WEALTHY.)

Butter ✖ 3 tablespoons

Blanched whole hazelnuts ✖ 1½ cups (7 ounces/200 grams)

Sugar ✖ 6 tablespoons

Dark chocolate ✖ 3½ ounces/100 grams, plus more for decoration

Milk chocolate ✖ 3½ ounces/100 grams

Freshly brewed strong espresso ✖ 4 tablespoons

Egg ✖ 1 large, beaten

Heavy cream ✖ 1¼ cups (10 fluid ounces/ 300 milliliters)

Lightly butter the ring of a 7-inch springform pan (you only need the ring part of the pan to keep the ingredients together as they firm up in the fridge; you won't be using the bottom part of the pan). Butter a serving platter or cake stand that is wide enough to hold the ring, and place the ring on the platter.

In a food processor, combine the hazelnuts and 4 tablespoons of the sugar and process until the mixture resembles coarse sand. Add 2 tablespoons of the butter and process until combined. Press this mixture firmly and evenly onto the serving plate, within the borders of the springform ring, and set aside.

Put the dark and milk chocolates in a small bowl and melt them, either in a microwave oven or over a saucepan of gently simmering water. Add the espresso and stir until well combined. Beat in the egg and the remaining 1 tablespoon butter and stir to combine. Let cool to room temperature.

In a large bowl, using a whisk or an electric mixer, beat the cream and remaining 2 tablespoons sugar until firm peaks form. Fold the whipped cream into the chocolate mixture and spoon the mixture over the hazelnut crust. Refrigerate until firm, at least 5 hours. When ready to serve, remove the springform ring and garnish with grated dark chocolate.

chocolate in italy

One reason Italian chocolate is so good is that Italians care so much about the purity of ingredients. Italy bans all genetically modified foods, but there is no better evidence for Italians' concern for quality than the country's long battle with the European Union (EU) over cocoa butter. According to Mario Piccialuti, director of AIDEPI, the Association of Italian Dessert and Pasta Manufacturers, "Since 2003, the EU permits chocolate to contain a certain percentage of vegetable oils, like palm, to substitute for the more expensive cocoa butter. However, Italy does not. By agreement, all members of AIDEPI use only 100 percent cocoa butter in their chocolates. Italian chocolate is 'pure chocolate.'"

Italy is home to some of the world's finest chocolate, from companies like Amedei, Caffarel, Domori, Ferrero, Majani, Novi, Pernigotti, Perugina, Peyrano, Vanini, and Venchi. A single region—Piedmont—is home to more master chocolatiers than Belgium and France combined!

Chocolate was originally enjoyed in Italy only as a drink, appearing in solid candy form much later. According to Gigi Padovani, one of Italy's leading chocolate experts, "The birthplace was Turin, in Piedmont. The first chocolate candies were created there between 1830 and 1850. The candies were called '*givu*,' Piedmontese dialect meaning cigarette butts, or little pieces of something. The candies were made from ground chocolate and sugar, which was rolled into a thin rod, and then cut into small round pieces."

FIVE WAYS TO SAVOR CHOCOLATE IN ITALY

When is the best time to eat chocolate? According to Giacomo Boidi, owner of Giraudi chocolates, "We Italians eat chocolate when we are happy, to celebrate, but we also eat it when we are sad, to cheer us up." He paused, then, eyes twinkling, added, "Italians also eat chocolate before making love, but it is wonderful after making love too!"

1. Experience Italy's most popular chocolate extravaganzas: the Turin Chocolate Festival, held in early March, or Eurochocolate, held in Perugia in October.
2. Visit one of Italy's chocolate factories, like Perugina, makers of *Baci,* and consider taking one of their fun-filled chocolate-making classes.
3. Be on the lookout for chocolates that are hard to find in the States, like Ferrero's *Kinder Sorpresa,* small chocolate eggs filled with puzzle pieces that assemble into a collectible toy; or their Pocket Coffee, little shots of real espresso coated in bittersweet chocolate.
4. While in Sicily, try Modica's stone-ground chocolate, made from a centuries-old method. In Palermo, order *torta sette veli* ("cake of the seven veils"), an elaborate multilayer chocolate cake and a specialty of Pasticceria Cappello.
5. When you're in Modena, in Emilia, visit Caffè-Pasticceria Gollini in the outlying town of Vignola, and have a slice of their *Torta Barrozzi,* a chocolate-espresso-nut cake made from a secret recipe.

ricotta pear cake

Torta ricotta e pere

SERVES 12

REGION: Campania

Ricotta e pere is one of the most popular, most frequently ordered desserts in Naples and on the Amalfi coast. Fluffy ricotta and pear custard between two moist layers of hazelnut sponge cake, this cool, refreshing dessert is a relative newcomer, created in the late 1990s by Salvatore De Riso—TV cooking show host, pastry shop owner, and cookbook author. Don't be put off by the length of the instructions. Each step is easy, and the result is a surprisingly light, superb summer dessert. It keeps beautifully in the refrigerator for up to five days, and freezes well. After six weeks in the freezer, it is just as wonderful as on day one.

FOR THE CAKE:

Whole hazelnuts ✖ 2 cups (6 ounces/170 grams), finely ground

00 flour ✖ 6 tablespoons (1²/₃ ounces/45 grams)

Eggs ✖ 6 large

Sugar ✖ ²/₃ cup (4¹/₂ ounces/130 grams)

Butter ✖ 7 tablespoons (3¹/₂ ounces/100 grams), melted

FOR THE PEARS:

2 Bartlett or William pears, at least 6 ounces/170 grams each, peeled, cored, and diced or thinly sliced

Sugar ✖ ¹/₂ cup (3¹/₂ ounces/100 grams)

Juice of 1 lemon

Cornstarch ✖ 2 teaspoons

Pear brandy ✖ 1 to 2 tablespoons

FOR THE SYRUP:

Sugar ✖ ¹/₃ cup (2¹/₄ ounces/65 grams)

Pear brandy ✖ 3 to 4 tablespoons

Make the cake: Preheat the oven to 350°F (180°C). Butter and lightly flour two 9¹/₂-inch (23.75 centimeters) springform pans.

Grind the hazelnuts and flour in a mini food processor until very fine.

In a large bowl, using an electric mixer with the whisk attachment, combine the eggs and sugar and beat on high speed for 15 minutes, until the mixture has quadrupled in volume. Gently fold in the hazelnuts and flour with a spatula until just combined. Then add in the butter. Divide the batter between the two prepared pans and bake for 10 to 12 minutes, until firm to the touch. Set aside.

Make the pears: In a small saucepan combine the pears, sugar, lemon juice, and cornstarch and simmer over medium-low heat until the pears are soft. Remove from the heat, stir in the brandy, and let cool to room temperature. Set aside.

Make the syrup: In a small saucepan, combine the sugar and ¹/₂ cup (4 fluid ounces/120 milliliters) water and bring to a boil. Stir in brandy.

Make the filling: In a large bowl, using an electric mixer, beat the ricotta, sugar, and vanilla for at least 5 minutes, until creamy.

Meanwhile, beat the cream until firm peaks form. Using a spatula, gently fold the whipped cream into the ricotta mixture. Fold in the cooled pear mixture.

Assemble the dessert: Remove one of the cake layers from the pan and place on a serving platter large enough to hold the outer ring of the springform pan. Brush the cake with one-half of the syrup to moisten it. Pile the filling in the center of the cake and put the springform ring back over the cake.

Gently spread the filling to the edges and then top with the second layer of cake. Brush the remaining syrup over the top. Cover with plastic wrap and put in the freezer until set, about 2 hours. Remove the springform ring and refrigerate until ready to serve.

FOR THE FILLING:

Ricotta cheese ✖ 17 ounces/430 grams

Sugar ✖ ¾ cup (5¼ ounces/150 grams)

Pure vanilla extract ✖ 1 tablespoon

Heavy cream ✖ ¾ cup (6 fluid ounces/ 180 milliliters)

no-bake pandoro layer cake

Dolce al pandoro

SERVES 10

REGION: Veneto

This delicious no-bake layer cake, filled with creamy *zabaglione,* chocolate, and nuts, is a specialty of 12 Apostoli, a restaurant in lovely Verona. The charming owner, Giorgio Gioco, taught me how to make it as he told stories about all the famous guests he's cooked for over the years, including Barbra Streisand, who liked this cake so much that during a TV interview, she said it was the best dessert she'd ever tasted in her life! Chef Gioco uses *pandoro,* a star-shaped briochelike aromatic cake, made by the Bauli company headquartered nearby.

Egg yolks ✖ 5 large

Sugar ✖ 5 tablespoons (2¼ ounces/ 65 grams)

Marsala wine ✖ ½ cup (4 fluid ounces/ 120 milliliters)

Heavy cream ✖ 1½ cups (12 fluid ounces/ 360 milliliters)

Pandoro, preferably Bauli brand (see Sources, page 203) ✖ 12 ounces/340 grams, crust removed, cut into thin slices

Dark chocolate ✖ 2 ounces/55 grams, finely grated

Mixed chopped nuts ✖ 1 cup (4 ounces/ 115 grams), toasted

4 crisp *amaretti* (almond cookies), crushed

Bring a pot of water to a boil. Combine the egg yolks and sugar in a metal or heat-resistant glass bowl and whisk until creamy. Set the bowl over the boiling water, without letting the bottom touch the water, and continue whisking. Gradually pour in the Marsala while continuing to whisk. Whisk until the custard triples in volume and is thick enough to coat the back of a spoon, about 10 minutes. Pour into a clean bowl and let cool to room temperature, then cover with plastic wrap and refrigerate the *zabaglione* until cold.

In a large bowl, using a whisk or electric mixer, beat the cream until firm peaks form. Pour half of the cold *zabaglione* into the whipped cream. Set the remaining *zabaglione* aside.

Spread one third of the *zabaglione*-cream mixture in a 7-inch (17-centimeter) circle in the center of a serving platter. Top with *pandoro* slices to form a single layer in the shape of a circle. Spread half of the remaining *zabaglione*-cream mixture on top of the *pandoro* and top with one quarter of the chocolate and nuts, reserving the rest for the top layer. Add another layer of *pandoro,* and spread the remaining *zabaglione*-cream mixture over it. Spoon the reserved *zabaglione* over the *zabaglione*-cream mixture and top with the remaining nuts and the amaretti. Scatter the remaining chocolate over the top.

This dessert is best served after a few hours, so the *pandoro* can absorb some of the *zabaglione*-cream mixture. If you refrigerate it, let it sit at room temperature for 1 hour before serving to release the *pandoro*'s natural butter flavors. Slice as you would a layer cake and serve.

Pandoro is sold in a distinctive lampshade-shaped box that children often play with as a toy hat. In America, real estate agents have been known to advise sellers to simmer apples and cinnamon in the kitchen to entice buyers. In Italy, they suggest setting *pandoro* on the radiator to release its aroma.

Walk through Verona, the home of Romeo and Juliet, during the Christmas season and you'll see pretty violet and pink boxes of *pandoro* displayed throughout the town in all kinds of unlikely shop windows, including bookstores, clothing emporiums, and gift boutiques. Were the delicate colors of the package chosen in honor of Juliet? Actually, no. The founder of the Bauli company, Ruggero Bauli, had three older sons working in different parts of the business, two in production and one as a lawyer. Out of fairness, he assigned to his only daughter, then just a youngster, the critical task of deciding *pandoro*'s package colors.

"instant" chocolate cake

Dolce torino

SERVES 4 TO 6

REGION: Piedmont

It tickles me that this recipe, which feels so ultra-modern, comes from an Italian cookbook written in 1891! This no-bake cake is not only incredibly delicious, but it's easy to make. Store-bought *savoiardi* ladyfinger cookies are dipped in liqueur, layered with chocolate, and then refrigerated until firm. *Pronto fatto,* it's done.

In a large bowl, using a whisk or electric mixer, beat the butter, confectioners' sugar, and egg yolk until very smooth and creamy. Set aside.

Put the chocolate and cream in a small bowl and melt the chocolate, either in a microwave oven or over a saucepan of gently simmering water. Let the chocolate mixture cool to room temperature, then stir it and the vanilla into the butter mixture. Set aside.

Combine the warm water and the granulated sugar in a shallow bowl and stir until the sugar dissolves. Stir in the liqueur, adding more sugar to taste.

Dip 4 of the *savoiardi*, one at a time, into the liquid. Be sure to moisten them well on all sides. Arrange the 4 liqueur-dipped *savoiardi* in a row, close together, on a serving plate. Spread with one third of the chocolate mixture.

Repeat the dipping and layering to make two more layers, spreading the last layer of chocolate mixture on top and around the sides of the stacked *savoiardi*. Sprinkle the top layer with pistachios or hazelnuts. Refrigerate for 3 hours, or until firm. Serve cold.

Butter 7 tablespoons (3½ ounces/100 grams)

Confectioners' sugar ✖ ½ cup (1¾ ounces/50 grams)

Egg yolk ✖ 1 large

Dark chocolate ✖ 3½ ounces/100 grams

Heavy cream ✖ 2 tablespoons

Pure vanilla extract ✖ ½ teaspoon

Warm water ✖ 5 tablespoons

Sugar ✖ 2 tablespoons, plus more to taste

Sweet liqueur, such as *alchermes* (page 182) ✖ 4 tablespoons

12 *savoiardi* (crisp ladyfingers)

Crushed nuts ✖ 2 tablespoons

zuccotto

SERVES 8 TO 10

REGION: Tuscany

entrare nello zuccotto del prete.

TO PUT ON THE PRIEST'S HAT. (AN EXPRESSION THAT MEANS GETTING TO THE HEART OF THE MATTER.)

Zuccotto, a specialty of Florence, is a dome-shaped dessert made by lining a bowl with slices of sponge cake, filling the center with something creamy, and then closing the bottom with more cake. Thanks to the magical gluing properties of sugar, the slices of cake meld together to form a solid outer crust. This is a terrific dessert to learn to make and a fun recipe to play with—no-bake, pretty, and very versatile.

Sugar ✕ ½ cup (3½ ounces/100 grams)

Boiling water ✕ ½ cup (4 fluid ounces/ 120 milliliters)

Liqueur, such as Maraschino, Kirsch, or *alchermes* (page 182) ✕ ¼ cup (2 fluid ounces/60 milliliters)

Store-bought pandoro, sponge or pound cake ✕ 12 to 16 ounces/340 to 450 grams, thinly sliced

Heavy cream ✕ 1¼ cups (10 fluid ounces/300 milliliters); or any flavor ice cream 2 pints (16 ounces/450 grams)

Confectioners' sugar ✕ ⅔ cup (2½ ounces/65 grams)

Ricotta cheese ✕ 2½ cups (1 pound 6 ounces/625 grams)

Milk or dark chocolate ✕ 3½ ounces/ 100 grams

Chopped candied orange peel or candied fruit ✕ ⅔ cup (4½ ounces/130 grams)

Mascarpone cheese ✕ 3 ounces/85 grams

Put the granulated sugar in a small bowl and add the boiling water. Stir until the sugar is dissolved, then stir in the liqueur.

Line a 2-quart (2-liter) bowl with plastic wrap and brush with the liqueur mixture. Line the bottom and sides of the bowl with most of the cake slices. Fill in any gaps with small pieces of cake.

In a large bowl, using a whisk or electric mixer, whip the cream until soft peaks form, then add the confectioners' sugar and whip until stiff. (If you're using ice cream, just let it soften a little at room temperature.) Fold in the ricotta. Divide the mixture roughly in half, in two different bowls.

Grate 1 ounce (30 grams) of the chocolate and stir it and the candied fruit into one portion of the ricotta mixture.

Grate or chop the remaining chocolate and combine it with the mascarpone in a small bowl. Heat, either in a microwave oven or over a saucepan of boiling water, until the chocolate melts. Stir the chocolate-mascarpone mixture into the second portion of the ricotta mixture.

Brush most of the liqueur mixture over the cake. The cake should be almost saturated. Set the rest of the liqueur mixture aside.

Spread the chocolate-mascarpone-ricotta mixture over the cake slices. Next, fill in the remaining area with the ricotta–candied fruit mixture. Brush the remaining cake slices with most of the remaining liqueur mixture and arrange them, liqueur side down, over the filling to cover it completely, trimming the cake slices to fit, if necessary. Brush the bottom of the slices with the remaining liqueur mixture. Cover with plastic wrap and refrigerate (or freeze if using ice cream) for at least 3 hours and up to 1 day.

Remove the top piece of plastic wrap. Invert the cake onto a platter, then remove the bowl and the remaining plastic wrap. Sprinkle with confectioners' sugar and serve.

summer tiramisù

Zuppa tartara

SERVES 4

REGION: **Northern Italy**

You'll love this dish—it's beautiful and takes just seconds to assemble using supermarket ingredients. *Savoiardi* (crisp ladyfingers) are layered with peach jam and sweetened ricotta. The whole thing firms up so nicely that you can slice it like pound cake, creating an effortless, virtually instant no-bake peach cake.

Zuppa tartara means "raw soup," because the ingredients aren't cooked. This dessert is so light and easy to make that it might surprise you to learn that the recipe comes from an 1890s cookbook, the famed *Science in the Kitchen and the Art of Eating Well* by Pellegrino Artusi.

In a medium bowl, combine the ricotta, sugar, and cinnamon and beat with a fork until smooth. Set aside.

In a shallow bowl, combine the jam with the warm water and the liqueur. Dip the *savoiardi*, a few at a time, into the mixture until they are nicely moistened. Place 4 on a serving plate, side by side, and spoon half of the ricotta mixture over them. Top with small dollops of extra jam. Repeat. Finish with final layer of dipped savoiardi and a final drizzle of preserves, or any of the remaining preserves liquid and bits.

Cover with plastic wrap and refrigerate for at least 1 hour. Serve cold.

Ricotta cheese ✖ 8 ounces/225 grams

Sugar ✖ 2 teaspoons

Pinch of ground cinnamon

Peach jam ✖ 4 heaping tablespoons

Warm water ✖ ¼ cup (2 fluid ounces/ 60 milliliters)

Sweet liqueur or rum ✖ 2 tablespoons

12 *savoiardi* (crisp ladyfingers)

pizza dolce

SERVES 8 TO 10

REGION: Abruzzo, especially Teramo

This is a decadently rich almond-chocolate layer cake: three layers of sponge cake,
each moistened with a different fabulous flavor, and each spread with chocolate-almond or vanilla
custard. Called "pizza" because of its round shape, this recipe was taught to me by an octogenarian chef,
Elio Pompa, who contributed so much to Italy's cuisine that he was awarded the title "*Cavaliere,*" a sort
of Italian knighthood.

FOR THE PASTRY CREAMS:

Egg yolks ✖ 8 large

Sugar ✖ ½ cup (3½ ounces/100 grams)

All-purpose flour ✖ ½ cup (2 ounces/
55 grams)

Milk ✖ 3 cups (24 fluid ounces/
720 milliliters)

Heavy cream ✖ 1 cup (8 fluid ounces/
240 milliliters)

Pure vanilla extract ✖ 2 teaspoons

Dark chocolate ✖ 1½ ounces/40 grams,
finely chopped

Unsweetened cocoa powder ✖ 1 tablespoon

Generous handful of chopped blanched
almonds

FOR THE CAKE LAYERS:

1 recipe Italian Sponge Cake (page 199),
prepared in a 10-inch spring form pan

Make the pastry creams: In a large bowl, combine the egg yolks and sugar and beat, using an electric mixer or whisk, until creamy and light yellow. Mix in the flour, 1 tablespoon at a time, until smooth. Set aside.

Put the milk, cream, and vanilla in a medium saucepan and heat over low heat until bubbles begin to appear at the edge of the pan. Do not boil. Remove from the heat and gradually beat the egg yolk mixture into the hot milk, making sure to beat until there are no lumps. Return the saucepan to low heat and cook, stirring constantly with a wooden spoon, until the mixture thickens, about 3 minutes. Do not overcook. The mixture should be thick, but not stiff. It will solidify as it cools.

Immediately remove the pan from the heat and pour three quarters of the mixture into one bowl and one quarter into another bowl. Add the chocolate, cocoa powder, and almonds to the smaller amount, stirring until the chocolate is melted.

Cover both bowls with plastic wrap, with the wrap touching the surface of the pastry cream so it doesn't form a skin, and refrigerate until cold, at least 4 hours.

Prepare the cake layers: Cool the cake to room temperature. Carefully slice off the top and bottom crusts and split the cake horizontally into 3 layers, with one layer slightly thicker than the other two. That will become the bottom layer.

Assemble the dessert:
Layer 1: Put the thicker layer of cake on a serving plate. In a small bowl, combine the hot espresso with 3 tablespoons sugar and stir until the sugar is dissolved. Add the rum then brush the syrup over the entire layer, soaking it well. Use all the syrup. Top with the chocolate-almond pastry cream, spreading it evenly.

Layer 2: Place another layer of cake over the chocolate-almond pastry cream. In a small saucepan, bring ⅓ cup (2½ fluid ounces/75 milliliters) water and ½ cup (3½ ounces/100 grams) sugar to a boil and stir until the sugar is dissolved and some of the liquid evaporates, about 2 minutes. Remove the syrup from the heat and stir in the *alchermes*. Set aside.

In a small bowl, combine ½ cup (4 fluid ounces/120 milliliters) hot water with ¼ cup (1¾ ounces/50 grams) of sugar and stir until the sugar is dissolved. Stir in the maraschino liqueur and brush half of the syrup over the cake. Reserve the other half of the syrup for the final layer. Wait about 2 minutes for the syrup to be absorbed, then drizzle half of the *alchermes* mixture over the cake in a spiral pattern.

Spread evenly with half of the cold vanilla custard (reserving the remaining half for the final layer). Coarsely chop half of the chocolate and scatter it over the custard.

Layer 3: Drizzle the remaining *alchermes* syrup in a spiral pattern over the final layer of cake. Place it, *alchermes* side down, onto the custard. Brush the cake with the remaining maraschino syrup. Use all the syrup. Cover with plastic wrap and refrigerate for 12 hours, or overnight, so the cake can absorb all the ingredients and moisten.

Just before serving, spread the top and sides with the remaining vanilla custard. Generously sprinkle the top and sides of the cake with the almonds, and garnish the top with the remaining chocolate, either shaved or finely chopped.

TO ASSEMBLE THE DESSERT:

Freshly brewed hot espresso ✖ ¾ cup (6 fluid ounces/180 milliliters)

Rum ✖ 4 tablespoons

Sugar

Alchermes (page 182) ✖ ½ cup (4 fluid ounces/120 milliliters)

Maraschino liqueur ✖ ½ cup (4 fluid ounces/120 milliliters)

Dark chocolate ✖ 4 ounces/115 grams

Chopped blanched almonds ✖ 1½ cups (6 ounces/170 grams)

CHAPTER FOUR

pies

CROSTATE

cocoa-nib jam tart

Crostata di marmellata con fave di cacao

SERVES 8

REGION: Piedmont

del vino il primo,
del caffè il secondo,
della cioccolata il fondo.

WINE FROM THE FIRST, COFFEE FROM THE SECOND, AND HOT CHOCOLATE FROM THE BOTTOM. (THE BEST WINE IS MADE FROM THE FIRST PRESS; THE SECOND CUP OF COFFEE IS BETTER BECAUSE THE FIRST IS WEAKER; AND THE BEST PART OF HOT CHOCOLATE IS AT THE BOTTOM OF THE MUG.)

There's a cute twist in this simple, no-fuss, chocolate tart crust. It's made with finely ground cocoa nibs. Cocoa nibs—little broken-up bits of toasted cocoa bean—are chocolate in its purest state.

Nibs are as chocolatey as chocolate can be, with nothing added—no sugar, no vanilla, no preservatives, just fabulous 100 percent pure chocolate. Here they are ground in a coffee grinder, creating a flourlike texture that gives the crust a deeply rich, full-of-chocolate flavor and aroma.

The crust comes together in minutes, and is more a batter than a true crust. You just blend, then spread into a tart pan, top with jam, and bake for 20 minutes. Simple, yet sophisticated. Apricot, pear, raspberry, and cherry jam go especially well with this rich chocolate crust—orange marmalade, too.

The recipe comes from one of Turin's renowned pastry chefs and chocolatiers, Marco Vacchieri. Be sure to stop by his shop on your next visit to Piedmont.

Cocoa nibs ✖ 1/2 cup (2 1/2 ounces/70 grams)

Butter ✖ 12 tablespoons (6 ounces/170 grams)

All-purpose flour ✖ 1 3/4 cups (8 1/2 ounces/240 grams)

Confectioners' sugar ✖ 1 cup (3 1/2 ounces/100 grams)

Eggs ✖ 2 large

Unsweetened cocoa powder ✖ 1 tablespoon

Jam or marmalade ✖ 1 cup (12 ounces/340 grams)

Grind the cocoa nibs in a coffee grinder until the texture resembles flour. Set aside.

Preheat the oven to 350°F (180°C). Lightly butter and flour a deep 9-inch (23-centimeter) round tart pan or springform cake pan.

In a medium bowl, using an electric mixer, beat the butter and confectioners' sugar until fluffy. Beat in the eggs until creamy. Add the cocoa nibs, cocoa powder, and flour and beat until well combined.

Spread three quarters of the batter in the bottom of the prepared pan and up the sides to a height of 1 inch (2.5 centimeters).

Spread the jam evenly in the bottom of the tart. Decorate with the remaining crust by piping it out with a pastry bag or thick plastic bag with a tip cut from the corner.

Bake for 20 minutes, or until the crust is firm. Cool to room temperature on a wire rack. Sprinkle with confectioners' sugar or cocoa powder and serve.

torta della nonna

SERVES 8

REGION: Tuscany, but popular throughout Italy

Torta della nonna, the charmingly named "Grandma's cake," is vanilla custard pie generously topped with pine nuts. One of Italy's most popular desserts, it's found in every region of Italy, in homes, restaurants, and pastry shops. This dessert is much, much better a day—or even two—after it's baked. It's served cold, so although quite rich, it's a fantastic summer dessert.

FOR THE FILLING:

Egg yolks ✖ 8 large

Sugar ✖ 1 cup (7 ounces/200 grams)

All-purpose flour ✖ 1 cup (4½ ounces/130 grams)

Milk ✖ 4 cups (32 fluid ounces/960 milliliters)

Pure vanilla extract ✖ 1½ tablespoons

Grated zest of ½ lemon

Pine nuts ✖ 1 cup (4¾ ounces/135 grams)

FOR THE CRUST:

All-purpose flour ✖ 3 cups (14 ounces/400 grams)

Cold unsalted butter ✖ 14 tablespoons (7 ounces/200 grams), sliced

Salt ✖ ¼ teaspoon

Confectioners' sugar ✖ 1¼ cups (4¼ ounces/120 grams)

Egg yolks ✖ 3 large

Pure vanilla extract ✖ 1½ tablespoons

Grated zest of ½ lemon

Make the filling: In a large bowl, combine the egg yolks and sugar and beat, using an electric mixer or whisk, until creamy and light yellow. Mix in the flour, 1 tablespoon at a time, until smooth.

Put the milk, vanilla, and lemon zest in a saucepan and cook over low heat until bubbles begin to form around the edge of the pan. Do not boil.

Remove from the heat and gradually whisk the egg yolk mixture into the hot milk, making sure to whisk until there are no lumps. Return to low heat and cook, stirring constantly with a wooden spoon, until the mixture thickens, about 3 minutes. Do not overcook. The mixture should be thick, but not stiff. It will solidify as it cools.

Immediately remove from the heat and pour into a bowl. Stir in ½ cup (2½ ounces/70 grams) of the pine nuts. Cover with plastic wrap, with the wrap touching the surface of the filling so it doesn't form a skin, and refrigerate until cold, at least 4 hours.

Make the crust: In a large bowl using your hands, or in a food processor, combine the flour, butter, and salt until the mixture resembles coarse sand. Mix in the confectioners' sugar, then add the egg yolks, vanilla, and lemon zest and knead until a dough forms. Cover the dough with plastic wrap and refrigerate for at least 1 hour.

Assemble the *torta*: Preheat the oven to 350°F (180°C). Lightly butter and flour a 10- to 11-inch (25- to 28-centimeter) round cake pan.

Roll out half of the dough into a large circle and press it into the bottom of the prepared pan, cutting any excess so it is flush with the top of the pan. Don't worry if it breaks apart; just press the pieces together in the pan. Using a fork, pierce the dough all over the bottom and sides of the crust. Pour the filling into the crust. Roll out the remaining dough, as thin as possible, to cover the top of the pan. Lay the dough over the top of the cake pan, overlapping the top edges a little. Cut away any excess dough so the crust is flat and flush with the edges. (Do not crimp the edge like with pie.)

Top the crust with the remaining ½ cup (2½ ounces/70 grams) pine nuts and bake for about 50 minutes, until the edges are golden. The filling inside will be very jiggly, but will solidify as it cools. Remove from the oven and cool to room temperature on a wire rack, then cover with plastic wrap and refrigerate. The *torta* is best served after 24 hours and stays fresh in the refrigerator for up to 1 week. Sprinkle generously with confectioners' sugar and serve cold.

olive oil–apple pie

Sfogliata di mele

SERVES 8

REGION: Abruzzo

*di maggio ciliege
per assaggio, di giugno
ciliege a pugno.*

IN MAY A MERE TASTE OF
CHERRIES, BY JUNE A FISTFUL.

This pie features a deeply flavorful, crisp crust filled with slow-cooked apples and dark chocolate. The crust is actually multiple thin layers of dough, like the French *millefeuille* puff pastry, but made with olive oil instead of butter. Between the layers is a sprinkling of aromatic cinnamon-sugar. Just the aroma of the sugar and cinnamon stick whirling in the food processor is enough to get your mouth watering. Be sure to use a stick of cinnamon, and not ready-ground. It really makes a big difference!

I wasn't going to include Italian apple pie in this book because I've always assumed that the American version can't be beat. Then I tasted this one, made by a spry grandmother in Teramo and changed my mind.

FOR THE FILLING:

Firm cooking apples, such as Rome Beauty or Empire ✖ 4 pounds (1.8 kilograms)

Sugar ✖ ½ cup (3½ ounces/100 grams)

Dark chocolate ✖ 1 ounce/30 grams, chopped

Chopped almonds ✖ ⅓ cup (1½ ounces/ 40 grams)

Grated zest of ½ lemon

FOR THE CRUST:

White wine ✖ 1½ cups (12 fluid ounces/ 360 milliliters)

Sugar ✖ 1 cup plus 2 tablespoons (8 ounces/ 225 grams)

All-purpose flour ✖ 1¾ cups (1 pound/ 455 grams)

Olive oil ✖ 1 cup (8 fluid ounces/ 240 milliliters)

Salt ✖ ½ teaspoon

Cinnamon ✖ 1 (2-inch/5-centimeter) stick

Make the filling: Peel, core, and slice the apples, then put them in a saucepan and toss with the sugar. Cook, covered, over low heat, for about 2 hours, stirring occasionally, until the consistency is like a thick applesauce. Let cool to room temperature, then stir in the chocolate, almonds, and lemon zest. Set aside.

Make the crust: Combine the wine and 2 tablespoons of the sugar in a small saucepan and heat over medium heat until the sugar dissolves. Put the flour on a work surface and make a well in the center. Put the oil, hot wine mixture, and salt in the well and, using a fork, gradually incorporate some of the flour into the liquid until a dough forms. Knead the dough by hand for about 10 minutes, until very elastic and smooth. (Alternatively, knead the dough by passing it through the thickest setting on a pasta maker until elastic and smooth.)

In a mini food processor or coffee grinder, process the remaining 1 cup sugar and the cinnamon stick until the cinnamon is pulverized and fully combined with the sugar. Divide into 4 portions and set aside.

Preheat the oven to 350°F (180°C). Lightly oil a 10-inch (25-centimeter) round cake pan.

Divide the dough into 5 portions, 3 for the bottom crust and 2 for the top crust. On a sheet of parchment paper or on a lightly oiled work surface, roll one portion of dough out to a thin circle just large enough to cover the bottom of the pan. (It does not come up the side of the pan as in traditional pies.) Drizzle with a little oil and sprinkle with one portion of the cinnamon-sugar.

Roll another portion of dough out into a thin disk and put it over the first layer. Drizzle with oil and another portion of the cinnamon-sugar. Top with a third circle of dough, then spread the apple filling over the dough. Sprinkle with cinnamon-sugar.

The top crust is two layers thick: Top the apple filling with a circle of dough, drizzle with oil, and sprinkle with the remaining cinnamon-sugar. Finish with a final layer of dough. Pierce the dough with a fork all along the edge of the pie to seal all the layers. (Note that the crust is flush with the edges of the pan, more like a cake than our traditional crimped pie-crusts.)

Bake for about 20 minutes, until the crust is golden brown.

italian hospitality

Italians are extraordinarily hospitable, friendly, and helpful. They are also fiercely proud of their culinary traditions, so it was great fun asking for their help in gathering recipes and learning to make them for this book.

One of my favorite experiences was in Teramo, a city in Abruzzo where a friend from Rome, Febo Cammarano, meticulously orchestrated three marvelous days for me—packed from early morning until late evening with fabulous foodie experiences. He arranged for me to learn desserts with folks as varied as author and cooking school teacher Rosita Di Antonio, to artisan *vin cotto* maker Ezio Di Giacomo and home cooks like Tiziana Ragusi who arranged a particularly charming encounter. She persuaded her mother-in-law, two friends, and even her own sixteen-year-old son, Roberto, to prepare different desserts simultaneously so that I could learn four recipes in the most concentrated time period. They were all super-organized and amazingly patient as I stopped each one of them several times for photos and questions.

This pie is one of the desserts from that session, prepared by Margherita Palumbi, Tiziana's mother-in-law, Roberto's grandmother.

cherry-ricotta pie

Crostata di visciole e ricotta

SERVES 8 TO 10

REGION: Lazio, especially Rome

Filled with fabulous, fluffy white ricotta and a layer of cherry marmalade, this pie is a Roman-Jewish specialty.

mangio le ciliegie per la prima volta in un anno.

I'M EATING CHERRIES FOR THE FIRST TIME IN A YEAR. (ITALIANS OFTEN MAKE A WISH WHEN EATING THE FIRST CHERRY OF THE SEASON.)

Preheat the oven to 350°F (180°C).

Shape about two thirds of the dough into a ball and roll it out into a circle large enough to line a 9-inch (23-centimeter) deep-dish pie pan. Fit it into the pan, bringing the dough up the sides about 2 inches (5 centimeters) high. Using a fork, pierce holes all over the bottom of the crust. Gently line the crust with aluminum foil, fill with uncooked dried beans or pie weights, and bake for about 6 minutes, until lightly golden. Cool to room temperature on a wire rack.

In a large bowl, using an electric mixer, beat the egg whites until frothy, then add the sugar and continue to beat until glossy and stiff peaks form. Fluff the ricotta a little with a fork, then fold it into the whites until combined.

Spread the cherry preserves in the bottom of the crust, then top with the ricotta mixture.

Roll out the remaining dough into a circle and set it over the filling. Bake for about 40 minutes, until the crust is golden. Cool to room temperature on a wire rack before serving.

1 recipe Pie Crust Dough (page 198)

Egg whites ✖ 3 large

Sugar ✖ ⅓ cup (2¼ ounces/65 grams), plus more to taste

Ricotta cheese ✖ 2¾ cups (1½ pounds/ 680 grams)

Wild or sour cherry preserves (*marmellata di visciole*) ✖ 1 cup (about 8 fluid ounces/ 240 milliliters)

no-fuss chocolate pear tart

SERVES 8

REGION: Piedmont and northern Italy

The moist, foolproof brownielike crust, made from crushed *amaretti*, comes together in a blink in a food processor yet looks and tastes pastry-shop perfect. Depending on the season, you can substitute other fresh fruit, such as peaches or apricots, for the pears.

quannu lu piru é maturu, cadi sulu.

WHEN THE PEAR IS RIPE, IT FALLS BY ITSELF.

Butter ✳ 5 tablespoons (10 ounces/ 280 grams)

Amaretti (almond cookies) ✳ 40 cookies (about 4 ounces/115 grams)

Eggs ✳ 3 large

Dark chocolate ✳ 3½ ounces/100 grams

Cream or milk ✳ 2 tablespoons

1 very ripe Bartlet or William pear

Sugar

Preheat the oven to 350°F (180°C). Butter an 8-inch (20-centimeter) round removable-bottom tart pan.

In a food processor, process the *amaretti* until very finely ground. Add the butter and eggs and process until well combined. Set aside.

Put the chocolate and cream in a small bowl and melt the chocolate, either in a microwave oven or over a saucepan of gently simmering water. Add to the *amaretti* mixture and process until well combined and creamy. Spread the mixture evenly in the prepared pan.

Peel, core, and thinly slice the pear lengthwise. Firmly press the core sides of the slices into the dough in a fan shape. Sprinkle the pear slices with sugar and bake for 35 to 40 minutes, until a toothpick inserted in center of the tart comes out clean. Serve warm.

neapolitan strawberry pie

Torta di fragole alla napoletana

SERVES 8

REGION: Campania

Just like strawberry soufflé—but without the anxiety. This specialty of Naples is served icy cold and makes a fabulous summer dessert.

Put the strawberries in a bowl, sprinkle with ¼ cup (1¾ ounces/ 50 grams) of the sugar, the wine, and lemon zest. Let macerate at room temperature for 1 hour to allow the flavors to mingle.

In a large bowl, combine the remaining ¼ cup (1¾ ounces/50 grams) sugar, the eggs, cream, and cinnamon and whisk until combined. Cut the *savoiardi* into 1-inch (2.5-centimeter) pieces and stir them into the mixture. Set aside for 30 minutes so the *savoiardi* can soften.

Meanwhile, preheat the oven to 360°F (185°C).

Roll half of the dough out into a circle large enough to line a 9-inch (23-centimeter) pie pan and press it in the pan. With a fork, pierce the bottom and sides of the crust. Roll the rest of the dough into a flat circle, then cut it into ½-inch (12-millimeter) strips for the lattice top.

Use a slotted spoon to spread the strawberries with a little of their liquid in the bottom crust. Pour the *savoiardi* mixture over the strawberries. Using the strips of dough, form a lattice over the top of the pie.

Bake for about 50 minutes, until the crust is golden. The center of the filling will be a little jiggly, but it will set as it cools. Cool to room temperature on a wire rack, then refrigerate until ready to serve. Serve cold.

Fresh strawberries ✳ 2 pounds (910 grams), washed, hulled, and sliced

Sugar ✳ ½ cup (3½ ounces/100 grams)

Dessert wine, such as Zibibbo or Marsala ✳ ½ cup (4 fluid ounces/120 milliliters)

Grated zest of 1 lemon

Eggs ✳ 6 large

Heavy cream ✳ 1 cup (8 fluid ounces/ 240 milliliters)

Ground cinnamon ✳ ½ teaspoon

Savoiardi (crisp ladyfingers) ✳ 8 cookies

1 recipe Pie Crust Dough (page 198)

honey-walnut chocolate glazed pie

dolce come il miele.
SWEET AS HONEY.

Bonissima

SERVES 8

REGION: Emilia-Romagna

Glazed with dark chocolate, this pie is filled with just three ingredients—walnuts, honey, and a splash of rum. Another example of how Italians only feature a few key ingredients to focus flavor!

Originally made without chocolate or rum, the dessert was modified in the seventeenth and eighteenth centuries to include those New World ingredients. This pie, called *bonissima*, is traditionally served during the Christmas holidays.

Near the Piazza Grande in Modena stands a life-size statue of a simply dressed woman that dates to 1468. Locals call her *la Bonissima*, "the Good One," in honor of a legendary wealthy medieval woman who gave all her riches to feed Modena's poor during a famine.

Plain bread crumbs ✕ 1 tablespoon

1 recipe Pie Crust Dough (page 198)

Coarsely chopped walnuts ✕ 1¾ cups (6 ounces/170 grams)

Honey ✕ 1 cup (8 fluid ounces/ 240 milliliters)

Rum ✕ ⅓ cup plus 1 tablespoon (3½ fluid ounces/95 milliliters)

Dark chocolate ✕ 3½ ounces/100 grams, chopped

Heavy cream ✕ ⅓ cup (2½ fluid ounces/ 75 milliliters)

Butter ✕ 1 teaspoon

Preheat the oven to 360°F (180°C).

Sprinkle the bread crumbs in the bottom of a 9-inch (23-centimeter) pie pan. Roll one ball of dough out into a circle large enough to line the pan and fit it in the pan. Using a fork, pierce the bottom and sides of the crust all over. Roll the second ball of dough out into a circle large enough to cover the pan.

In a medium bowl, combine the walnuts, honey, and rum and stir until combined. (The filling mixture will be liquidy, but will soak into the crust as the pie bakes.) Pour the filling into the bottom crust and set the top crust over the filling. Do not crimp the edges, but rather cut off the crusts flush with the edge of the pan. Bake for about 40 minutes, until the crust is golden. Cool to room temperature on a wire rack.

Put the chocolate in a small heatproof bowl. In a small saucepan, heat the cream until very warm but not boiling, then pour it over the chocolate, stirring until the chocolate melts. Stir in the butter. Let cool to room temperature, then spread the glaze over the top of the pie.

Serve at room temperature.

honey-nut spice pie

Spongata

SERVES 8 TO 10

REGION: Emilia-Romagna

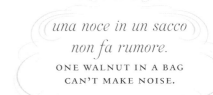

With a moist, nutty spongelike center and fragrant hints of wine and spices, this must-try pie was a favorite of composer Giuseppe Verdi. The recipe can be found in fourteenth-century Italian cookbooks. Food historians think it was either brought to Italy by the Jews or is based on an ancient Roman recipe for spiced bread. *Spongata* comes from the word *spugna*, or "sponge," and refers to the consistency of the filling and the tiny holes poked into the crust's surface. It may sound like a drawback, but one of the fun things about the filling is the fact that it's traditionally left to mellow for a few days before baking. Anticipation is a wonderful feeling, especially when it comes to sweets. But be warned: Don't taste the filling before you bake it. Oh, there's nothing in it that you can't eat raw, but if you taste it, you'll eat it all and there won't be anything left for the pie!

Put the *amaretti* in a food processor and process until finely ground. Add the bread crumbs, almonds, walnuts, and pine nuts and pulse until the nuts are coarsely ground. Add the raisins, citron, cinnamon, nutmeg, and cloves and pulse until combined. Set aside.

Bring a pot of water to a boil and place a medium glass bowl over the water. When the water boils, add the honey to the bowl and stir until it liquefies. Add the ground *amaretti* mixture and simmer for 5 minutes. Remove from the heat and stir in the wine. Cover with plastic wrap and set aside in a cool, dry place for 2 to 15 days, stirring the filling mixture each day.

Preheat the oven to 400°F (200°C). Roll one half of the dough out into a circle large enough to line an 8-inch (20-centimeter) tart or pie pan and fit it in the pan.

Spoon in the filling (it will only come halfway up the pie pan) and drizzle 1 tablespoon of the oil over it. Roll out the remaining dough and place it over the filling, but do not crimp the edges as with traditional American pies. The edges should meet flush, so trim the edges of the pie to cut away any excess dough. Using a fork or skewer, pierce the top crust, then brush the top with the remaining 1 tablespoon oil.

Bake for about 25 minutes, until golden. Cool to room temperature on a wire rack, then sprinkle with confectioners' sugar and serve. This pie keeps well for several days.

Amaretti (almond cookies) ✖ 6 cookies

Plain dried bread crumbs ✖ ¼ cup (1 ounce/30 grams)

Blanched whole almonds ✖ ⅔ cup (3½ ounces/100 grams), toasted

Walnuts ✖ ½ cup (1¾ ounces/50 grams), toasted

Pine nuts ✖ ⅓ cup (1½ ounces/40 grams), toasted

Raisins ✖ ⅓ cup (2 ounces/55 grams)

Candied citron or candied orange peel ✖ ¼ cup (2 ounces/55 grams) or grated zest of 1 orange

Pinch of ground cinnamon

Pinch of freshly grated nutmeg

Pinch of ground cloves

Honey ✖ 1 cup (8 fluid ounces/ 240 milliliters)

White wine ✖ ½ cup (4 fluid ounces/ 120 milliliters)

1 recipe Pie Crust Dough (page 198)

Olive oil ✖ 2 tablespoons

Confectioners' sugar

bird's beak pie

Torta coi becchi

SERVES 8

REGION: Tuscany, especially the city of Lucca

Rice pudding slow-cooked to creamy perfection, then baked with dark chocolate, pine nuts, and hints of orange—this not only tastes astonishing, but also has an adorable crust and cute double-entendre name.

Becchi literally means "bird beaks," and the name comes from the fact that the dough around the pie is pinched into thick beak-looking points. But *becco* is also slang for "cuckold" in Tuscany, where this pie is always served with a wink.

Milk ✖ 5 cups (40 fluid ounces/1.2 liters)

Long-grain rice ✖ 1 cup (7½ ounces/ 215 grams)

Sugar ✖ ¾ cup (5¼ ounces/150 grams)

Salt

Dark chocolate ✖ 3½ ounces/100 grams, chopped

Raisins ✖ ⅓ cup (2 ounces/55 grams)

Pine nuts ✖ ½ cup (2½ ounces/70 grams), toasted in a dry pan

Diced candied orange or citron peel ✖ ¼ cup (2 ounces/55 grams) or grated zest of ½ orange

Unsweetened cocoa powder ✖ 2 tablespoons

Orange liqueur, such as Aurum or Grand Marnier ✖ ¼ cup (2 fluid ounces/ 60 milliliters)

Butter for the pan

1 recipe Pie Crust Dough (page 198)

Egg yolks ✖ 3 large, beaten

Combine the milk, rice, sugar, and salt to taste in a medium saucepan and bring to a low boil. Reduce the heat to low and simmer, covered, stirring occasionally, until the rice is very soft, about 30 minutes. Add more milk, if needed; the rice should be loose. Add the chocolate to the hot rice mixture, stirring until melted. Stir in the raisins, pine nuts, candied orange peel, cocoa powder, and liqueur. Let cool to room temperature.

Preheat the oven to 350°F (180°C). Butter a 9-inch (23-centimeter) pie pan.

Roll the dough out into a large circle and cut off four or five 1-inch- (2.5-centimeter-) wide strips of dough for topping the pie. Fit the dough into the prepared pan. Fold the edges of the dough and shape into thick bird beaks by pinching the dough between your thumb and forefinger; space the beaks around the edge so that each slice will feature one centered beak.

Stir the egg yolks into the cooled rice mixture. If the mixture is too thick, add a little more milk. Spoon the mixture into the crust and top with the strips of dough. Bake for about 50 minutes, until the crust is golden. Cool to room temperature on a wire rack and serve.

CHAPTER FIVE

freezer desserts

SEMIFREDDI E GRANITE

spumone with homemade hazelnut brittle

Spumone al croccante

SERVES 6

REGION: Throughout Italy

In the United States, *spumone* has come to mean ice cream in three layers—strawberry, vanilla, and pistachio—for the colors of the Italian flag. Not in Italy. There, *spumone* is the general name for a category of semifrozen whipped-cream desserts.

Once I tasted this embarrassingly simple-to-make four-ingredient treat, taught to me by Sarah Scaparone, an Italian journalist, I gave away my ice cream maker. In fact, it is because of this recipe that there are no gelato recipes in this book. Why bother with a special freezing contraption when you can enjoy a creamy frozen delight without one? Plus, just like with ice cream, you can vary it in thousands of ways, and—unlike many *semifreddo* recipes—it contains no raw eggs. Try it once, and I guarantee this will become one of your favorite go-to desserts.

Put ¼ cup (1¾ ounces/50 grams) of the sugar in a small saucepan and heat over medium heat until the sugar begins to melt and turn light golden. Remove from the heat and stir in the nuts. Working quickly, before the mixture hardens, spread the candied nuts onto a baking sheet lined with parchment paper. Let cool to room temperature, then break into tiny bits. Set aside.

Bring a pot of water to a low boil over medium heat. Combine the egg yolks and the remaining ½ cup (3½ ounces/100 grams) sugar in a metal or glass heat-resistant bowl and whisk until creamy and light yellow. Then set the bowl over the boiling water, without letting the bottom touch the water, and continue to whisk until the mixture is thick. Remove the bowl from the pot and stir in three quarters of the candied hazelnut bits. This is the *spumone* mixture.

In a large bowl, whip the cream until firm peaks form. Fold the whipped cream into the cold *spumone*.

Line a small (4-by-8-inch/20-by-11-centimeter) loaf pan with plastic wrap. Spoon the *spumone* into the pan and place in the freezer for about 4 hours, until firm. Turn out onto a serving plate, remove the plastic wrap, and garnish with the remaining candied hazelnut bits. Slice and serve.

Sugar ✖ ¾ cup (5¼ ounces/150 grams)

Finely crushed hazelnuts ✖ ⅓ cup (2 ounces/55 grams)

Egg yolks ✖ 4 large

Heavy cream ✖ 1½ cups (12 fluid ounces/360 milliliters)

UN ALTRO MODO

Almond or Pistachio Brittle *Spumone*: Substitute almonds or pistachios for the hazelnuts.

Candy Jar *Spumone*: Instead of making brittle, substitute store-bought candy, such as chopped Baci, caramels, *gianduiotti*, or *torrone*. *Spumone* is the perfect place for anything in your candy jar!

Chestnut Chocolate *Spumone*: Add 1½ ounces (45 grams) finely chopped milk or dark chocolate and ⅔ cup (3¼ ounces/90 grams) minced roasted or candied chestnuts when you fold in the whipped cream.

Cookie Crunch: Fold 1 cup (8 fluid ounces/240 milliliters) chopped cookies in with the whipped cream.

Fruit Crunch: Fold in 1 cup (about 5¼ ounces/150 grams) finely diced fruit in with the whipped cream. Bananas work especially well with the hazelnut.

fruit and spice spumone

Spumone al paneforte

SERVES 6

REGION: Throughout Italy

Panforte, a spicy mix of fruit and nuts, is one of my favorite Italian treats. Available here online or in gourmet shops, I always have it on hand. I not only like to serve small wedges for dessert, but also use it as an ingredient. It gives me a chance to add tasty Italian nuts and fruit to cake batter, pudding, fresh fruit salad, and this delicious, simple frozen delight.

Sugar ✕ ½ cup (3½ ounces/100 grams)

Egg yolks ✕ 4 large

Panforte, preferably Corsini brand (see sources) ✕ 6 ounces/170 grams, chopped

Heavy cream ✕ 1½ cups (12 fluid ounces/ 360 milliliters)

Bring a pot of water to a low boil over medium heat. Combine the sugar and egg yolks in a metal or glass heat-resistant bowl and whisk until creamy and light yellow. Set the bowl over the boiling water, without letting the bottom touch the water, and continue to whisk until all the sugar is dissolved and the mixture is thick. Remove the bowl from the pot and let cool to room temperature. Stir in about three quarters of the *panforte*. This is the *spumone* mixture.

In a large bowl, whip the cream until firm peaks form. Fold the whipped cream into the *spumone*. Line a small (4-by-8-inch/10-by-20-centimeter) loaf pan with plastic wrap. Spoon the *spumone* into the pan and place in the freezer for about 4 hours, until firm. Turn out onto a serving plate, remove the plastic wrap, and garnish with the remaining *panforte*. Slice and serve.

in italy

Panforte, "strong bread," a Tuscan specialty especially from Siena, is made with candied and dried fruits, almonds, and honey. It's coated with a thin, white, edible wafer and topped with confectioners' sugar. It's especially popular during the Christmas holidays. There are various versions of *panforte*, including *panforte nero*, which is covered in chocolate. A similar Christmas sweet is *pampepato*, "pepper bread," a specialty of Umbria. The white edible wafer that coats both sides of *panforte* is also used to make other sweets and is sold in Italian grocery stores. Curiously, it is also sold in pharmacies. The wafers are packaged as round disks, of various sizes, meant to wrap around medicines to make them easier to swallow.

strawberry spumone

SERVES 4

REGION: Throughout Italy

With this basic recipe, you can create countless variations substituting virtually any fruit for the strawberries. Try raspberries, cherries, ripe peaches, or bananas.

Line a small (4-by-8-inch/10-by-20-centimeter) loaf pan or other container with plastic wrap so it hangs over the edges a few inches on all sides.

In a large bowl, whip the cream until firm peaks form. Set aside.

In a mini food processor or blender, combine the strawberries and lemon juice and puree until almost completely smooth. Stir in the sugar and fold the mixture into the whipped cream.

Spoon into the prepared pan, cover with the overhanging plastic wrap, and put in the freezer for at least 4 hours, until firm.

Pick up the edges of the plastic wrap and remove the molded *spumone*. Place on a serving plate, slice, garnish with fresh strawberries, and serve.

Heavy cream ✳ 1¼ cups (10 fluid ounces/ 300 milliliters)

Fresh strawberries ✳ 9 ounces/255 grams, plus more for garnish

Juice of 1 lemon

Confectioners' sugar ✳ 1 cup plus 2 tablespoons (4 ounces/115 grams)

semifreddo al limone

SERVES 8

REGION: Throughout Italy

Light as a cloud, not too sweet, and quick to make, this dessert is elegant enough for fancy dinner parties but simple enough for a midweek treat. The basic recipe can be varied in hundreds of ways; this version is like homemade lemon ice cream, but with no need for an ice cream maker.

Eggs ✳ 5 large, separated

Sugar ✳ ½ cup (3½ ounces/100 grams)

Grated zest of 1 lemon

Juice of 2 lemons

Unflavored gelatin ✳ 1 envelope (¼ ounce/ 7 grams)

Heavy cream ✳ 1 cup (8 fluid ounces/ 240 milliliters)

Line a small (4-by-8-inch/10-by-20-centimeter) loaf pan or 4-cup (32 fluid ounces/960 milliliters) mold with plastic wrap.

Bring a saucepan of water to a boil. Put the egg yolks and sugar in a large bowl and whisk until frothy. Remove the saucepan from the heat and put the bowl over the hot water. Whisk until the mixture is light yellow and creamy. Add the lemon zest, lemon juice, and gelatin and whisk until combined.

In a large bowl, beat the egg whites until stiff peaks form. Fold the whites into the lemon mixture.

In another large bowl, whip the cream until firm peaks form, then fold it into the lemon mixture. Spoon into the prepared mold and freeze for about 2 hours, until set. Turn out onto a serving platter, remove the plastic wrap, and serve immediately.

UN ALTRO MODO

Raspberry Lemon *Semifreddo*: Fold in a handful of fresh or frozen raspberries with the whipped cream.

Chocolate Lemon *Semifreddo*: Fold in some grated dark chocolate with the whipped cream.

Spiked Lemon Almond *Semifreddo*: Fold in a few tablespoons of limoncello, some chopped almonds, and 6 to 8 crushed *amaretti* (crisp almond cookies) with the whipped cream.

lemon granita, just like in italy

Granita al limone come quella del bar

SERVES 6

REGION: Sicily

I rushed down to the kitchen as soon as I woke up. In the freezer, just as promised, was a picture-perfect bowl of lemon granita like you'd get in a bar in Italy. Amazing considering that I hadn't had to scrape, stir, or do a thing. It was like magic. The granita was smooth, without ice crystals, and I didn't need an ice cream maker. Unbelievable.

Through trial and error and sheer persistence, Ornella Mirelli, one of my favorite Italian food bloggers, had discovered that a little honey, a whirl with an electric mixer, and a freezer set at medium is all it takes for ideal lemon granita.

Bring 1½ cups (12 fluid ounces/360 milliliters) water, the sugar, and lemon zest to a boil, then lower the heat and cook at a low boil for 3 to 4 minutes. Remove from the heat and add the lemon juice and honey. Using an electric mixer or immersion blender, beat the mixture for 1 minute.

Pour the mixture into a freezer-safe glass or plastic container and freeze overnight or for at least 12 hours.

The granita stays soft for up to 1 week in the freezer, but to keep it longer, store the container in a resealable plastic bag.

Sugar ✕ 1½ cups (10½ ounces/300 grams)

Grated zest of 1 lemon

Freshly squeezed lemon juice ✕ 1 cup (8 fluid ounces/240 milliliters)

Honey ✕ 1 heaping tablespoon

During the hot summers, many Sicilians enjoy a cool breakfast brioche sandwich filled with granita or gelato and topped with a dollop of whipped cream. These special brioche rolls, called *brioche con il tuppo,* have a little rounded tip on top, and also go by the colorful nickname *brioscia a minna,* brioche with a breast.

licorice granita

SERVES 8
REGION: Calabria

Real licorice—I don't mean the sweet red gummy stuff—is very popular in Italy, not only as a candy but also as a flavoring for both savory and sweet foods. I especially love licorice in granita because its strong flavor is toned down a notch by the icy coldness. Plus you can control the sweetness to suit your tastes. Small, hard Italian licorice candies quickly melt in boiling water to create this chic treat.

Unsweetened hard licorice candies, such as Amarelli ✕ ¾ ounce/20 grams

Raw or turbinado sugar ✕ ⅔ cup (4½ ounces/130 grams)

Bring 4 cups/960 milliliters water to a boil in a medium saucepan. Add the licorice candies and sugar and simmer until the sugar and licorice are dissolved, about 4 minutes. Let cool to room temperature, then pour into a metal or freezer-safe glass container. Freeze for about 4 hours, breaking up the ice crystals with a fork or whisk every 30 to 40 minutes. Scrape with a fork or spoon and serve in wineglasses or dessert cups.

coffee granita

SERVES 4

REGION: Sicily

Making granita couldn't be simpler. Put the mixture in the freezer, break up the ice crystals every hour or so until they stay crystallized, and enjoy.

Granita is a Sicilian invention. In the past, during the warm months, noble and wealthy families of Sicily kept *case neviere*—snow houses—to store the snow gathered from the top of Mount Etna. Each section of Sicily has its own particular specialty granita. Coffee granita is typical of Messina, where it's often served with a generous dollop of whipped cream.

In a small saucepan, bring ½ cup (4 fluid ounces/120 milliliters) water to a boil, then stir in the granulated sugar and vanilla bean. Bring back to a boil, then lower the heat and simmer for 2 minutes. Remove from the heat and stir in the coffee. Let cool to room temperature.

Taste, and add more granulated sugar or coffee, if you like. Remove the vanilla bean and pour into a metal or freezer-safe glass container and freeze for 3 to 4 hours, breaking up the ice crystals and stirring with a fork or whisk every 30 to 40 minutes.

If parts have become solid, scrape the granita with a fork or grapefruit spoon. Serve topped with whipped cream and confectioners' sugar, if you like.

UN ALTRO MODO

Caffè Latte Granita: Substitute ½ cup (4 fluid ounces/120 milliliters) whole milk for the water, but bring just to a low, not full boil.

Espresso Corretto Granita: When you stir in the espresso, add ¼ cup (2 fluid ounces/60 milliliters) grappa or sambuca or ½ cup (4 fluid ounces/120 milliliters) amaretto or other sweet liqueur.

Sugar ✂ ⅓ cup (2¼ ounces/65 grams)

1 vanilla bean, split and scraped

Freshly brewed hot espresso or strong coffee ✂ 1 cup (8 fluid ounces/240 milliliters)

Whipped cream and confectioners' sugar, optional

almond granita

Granita alle mandorle

SERVES 4

REGION: Sicily

Rich but not heavy, and wonderfully creamy, this is a simple two-ingredient summer treat that is ideal for vegetarians (and vegans, if you use sugar instead of honey) or anyone who is lactose intolerant.

Almond paste (see Note) ✳ 7 ounces/
200 grams, diced

Honey or sugar

Mix the almond paste to taste with 2 cups (16 fluid ounces/480 milliliters) water in a blender and process until the almond paste is completely incorporated. Taste and add honey or sugar, if you like.

Pour into a shallow metal or freezer-safe glass container and freeze for about 3 hours, breaking the ice crystals with a fork every 30 to 40 minutes.

To serve, scrape the mixture with a fork until it resembles a slushy, and serve immediately.

NOTE: If you can't get quality almond paste, use freshly made almond milk, either homemade or from a health food store. If you use almond milk, there's no need to add water.

UN ALTRO MODO

Almond Coffee Granita: Serve the granita topped with a sprinkle of instant coffee or espresso powder.

Pistachio Granita: Substitute pistachios for the almond paste. Using a mortar and pestle, grind the same weight of pistachios until a paste forms, then follow the directions above.

Sorbetlike Almond Granita: Many Sicilian gelato shops add stiffly beaten egg whites to almond granita to make it creamier and more sorbetlike. To make it: After the granita has been in the freezer for 3 hours, beat 2 large egg whites until stiff peaks form, fold the whites into the granita, and freeze for another 40 minutes. Scrape with a fork and serve.

asti spumante granita

SERVES 6

REGION: Piedmont

This is a sophisticated yet simple granita made with Asti Spumante, a sparkling white dessert wine, that adds a lovely grape aroma and taste. Plus, the little bit of alcohol helps keep the mixture from freezing as hard as the usual granita, so it's easier to serve. You can substitute just about any fruit for the strawberries. Try peaches, cantaloupe, raspberries, or even a combination—all are delicious with Asti.

*pane coi buchi,
formaggio compatto,
e vino che salti in faccia.*

BREAD WITH HOLES, COMPACT
CHEESE, AND WINE THAT JUMPS
TO YOUR FACE (SAID WHEN EATING
CRUSTY BREAD, AGED CHEESE AND
SPARKLING WINE).

Put the sugar, strawberries, and 1 cup (8 fluid ounces/240 milliliters) of the wine in a blender or food processor and blend until smooth, about 30 seconds. Pour in the remaining wine and pulse once or twice to combine.

Pour into a shallow freezer-safe glass container and freeze for about 4 hours, breaking up the ice crystals with a fork every 30 to 40 minutes. Scrape with a fork or grapefruit spoon and serve in wineglasses or dessert cups.

Sugar ✕ ¾ cup (5 ¼ ounces/150 grams)

Fresh strawberries ✕ 1 quart/960 milliliters

Asti Spumante ✕ 2 cups (16 fluid ounces/ 480 milliliters)

semifreddo al torrone

SERVES 8

REGION: Throughout Italy

Creamy white, studded with bits of chewy *torrone*, this icy cold treat is served topped with warm melted chocolate. As lovely as it is luscious, it comes together quickly without any special equipment.

Eggs ✳ 3 large, separated

Sugar ✳ ½ cup (3½ ounces/100 grams)

Heavy cream ✳ 3 cups plus 2 tablespoons (25 fluid ounces/750 milliliters)

Torrone (Italian nougat) ✳ 12 ounces/ 340 grams, cut into small cubes

Dark chocolate ✳ 2 ounces/55 grams

Line a small (4-by-8-inch/10-by-20-centimeter) loaf pan or 4-cup (32 fluid ounces/960 milliliters) mold with plastic wrap.

In a large bowl, with an electric mixer, beat the egg yolks and sugar together until light yellow and fluffy.

In a separate large bowl, whip all but 2 tablespoons of the cream until firm peaks form, then fold the whipped cream into the egg yolk mixture.

In another large bowl, with clean and dry beaters, beat the egg whites until stiff peaks form, then fold the whites, along with the *torrone*, into the egg yolk mixture. Spoon the mixture into the prepared pan and freeze for about 4 hours, until firm.

Just before serving, put the chocolate and remaining 2 tablespoons cream in a small bowl and melt the chocolate, either in a microwave oven or over a saucepan of gently simmering water. Unmold the *semifreddo* onto a serving plate and remove the plastic wrap. Serve it immediately, sliced and topped with the chocolate.

torrone

Throughout Italy there are many variations of *torrone,* a nougat candy made of nuts, honey, and egg whites. Each region's version highlights its local ingredients, such as pistachio nuts, chocolate, liqueurs, or candied fruits. *Torrone* can be hard or soft, large or small, and even comes in small bite-sized pieces called *torroncini.* There are also chocolate-covered varieties.

Since at least the early Renaissance, *torrone* has been one of the traditional sweets served at Christmas and for special occasions, particularly weddings. The menu for the wedding banquet for Bianca Maria Visconti and Francesco Sforza, celebrated in Cremona in 1441, lists a sweet made of almonds, honey, and egg whites sculpted to look like the town's municipal tower, called *Torrione*. According to tradition, the name *torrone* comes from that tower.

hazelnut chocolate semifreddo

Semifreddo al gianduia

SERVES 6

REGION: Piedmont, and popular throughout Italy

Here in the States we're big on combining peanut butter and chocolate, but in Italy one of the most popular pairings is hazelnut and chocolate, a creamy blend called *gianduia*. It's worth a quick Internet search to find this amazingly aromatic and velvety smooth chocolate. It's great eaten plain, or in any recipes calling for chocolate, especially this one.

Egg whites ✼ 2 large

Sugar ✼ 2 tablespoons

Heavy cream ✼ ½ cup (4 fluid ounces/ 120 milliliters)

Gianduia chocolate ✼ 6 ounces/170 grams, melted

Line a small (4-by-8-inch/10-by-20-centimeter) loaf pan or 6 individual freezer-safe cups with plastic wrap.

In a medium bowl, beat the egg whites until stiff peaks form, then beat in 1 tablespoon of the sugar.

In another medium bowl, whip the cream until firm peaks form, then whip in the remaining 1 tablespoon sugar. Fold the egg whites into the whipped cream until combined, then gently fold in the melted chocolate until just combined. Do not overmix. Pour the mixture into the prepared pan or cups and freeze for about 3 hours, until very firm.

To serve, unmold onto a large serving platter or individual plates, remove the plastic wrap, and top with either shaved or melted *gianduia* chocolate.

rosemary semifreddo

SERVES 8

REGION: Campania and popular throughout Italy

"Close your eyes. Taste. It's like eating creamy ice cream while strolling through a field of rosemary, yes?" asks Giovanni Marzano, chef at the Grand Hotel Vesuvio, as I try a spoonful of this aromatic creamy bliss.

"Yes!"

Line a small (4-by-8-inch/10-by-20-centimeter) loaf pan or 4-cup (32 fluid ounces/960 milliliters) mold or 8 individual ½-cup (4 fluid ounces/120 milliliters) ramekins or molds with enough plastic wrap to extend over the sides.

Put ½ cup (3½ ounces/100 grams) of the sugar and 1 cup (8 fluid ounces/240 milliliters) water in a small saucepan and bring to a boil. Add the rosemary, lower the heat to medium, and cook for 15 minutes, until light green and fragrant. Remove from the heat, remove and discard the rosemary, sprinkle in the gelatin, and stir to combine. Let cool to room temperature.

In a medium heat-proof bowl set over a pot of gently boiling water, with an electric mixer, beat the egg yolks, the remaining ¼ cup (1¾ ounces/50 grams) sugar, and the honey until light and creamy, at least 5 minutes. Cool to room temperature.

Meanwhile, in a large bowl, whip the cream until firm peaks form. Gently fold the whipped cream and rosemary syrup into the egg yolk mixture until just combined. Pour into the prepared pan and cover with plastic wrap. Freeze until firm, about 4 hours if using one mold or 1 hour if using individual molds. Unmold onto a large serving platter or individual plates, remove the plastic wrap, and serve immediately.

Sugar ✳ ¾ cup (5¼ ounces/150 grams)

Fresh rosemary sprigs ✳ 2 large

Unflavored gelatin ✳ 1 envelope (¼ ounce/7 grams)

Egg yolks ✳ 4 large

Honey ✳ 2 tablespoons

Heavy cream ✳ 2 cups (16 fluid ounces/480 milliliters)

CHAPTER SIX

spoon
sweets

DOLCI AL CUCCHIAIO

winter fruit salad

Macedonia invernale

SERVES 10 TO 12

REGION: Throughout Italy

This is a terrific no-cook, no-fuss dessert that's very popular with
home cooks in Italy, but not very well known in the United States. Mix
your favorite dried fruits with nuts, chopped chocolate, and any candy you
have on hand. Add some orange juice and a splash of liqueur and pass the
spoons. It's a little like a deconstructed fruit cake—only scrumptious and striking—
especially if you include colorful dried fruit like strawberries, cherries, and apricots.

In a resealable plastic bag or plastic container with a lid, combine
the dried fruit, nuts, *torrone*, dark and milk chocolates, *amaretti*, and
candied orange peel. Seal and set aside in a cool, dry place for up to
3 months.

One hour before serving, add enough orange juice to moisten the fruit
mixture. Just before serving, add liqueur to taste, if you like. Serve in
wineglasses, topped with a dollop of mascarpone cheese or whipped
cream.

2 handfuls assorted dried fruit, chopped

2 handfuls assorted chopped nuts

1 handful soft *torrone* (Italian nougat candy),
or assorted leftover candy bars, chopped

1 handful dark chocolate, chopped

1 handful milk chocolate, chopped

10 *amaretti* (crisp almond cookies) or other
cookies, coarsely chopped

A little candied orange peel, minced

Freshly squeezed orange juice

Italian liqueur such as limoncello or amaretto

Mascarpone cheese or whipped cream

award-winning parmesan panna cotta with pears

Panna cotta al grana padana e pere

SERVES 6

REGION: Tuscany

al contadino non far sapere quanto è buono il cacio con le pere.

DON'T LET THE FARMER KNOW HOW DELICIOUS CHEESE AND PEARS ARE. (A TUSCAN EXPRESSION, SAID WHENEVER PEARS AND CHEESE ARE SERVED.)

Parmesan cheese adds a lovely salty-savory touch to *panna cotta*. A hint of thyme adds lovely aroma as well as an additional savory sweetness. The pears, simmered in Tuscany's famed Chianti wine, tie both together in a perfectly calibrated dessert.

I wanted a mix of sources for the recipes in this book, so I reached out to gray-haired grannies, hip foodies, bloggers, and even winners of Italian amateur cooking contests. This delightful prizewinning dessert was created by a young Tuscan carpenter, Roberto Gracci.

FOR THE PANNA COTTA:

Milk ✕ 2 cups (16 fluid ounces/ 480 milliliters)

Parmesan cheese ✕ 2 ounces/55 grams, grated

Sugar ✕ ⅓ cup (2¼ ounces/65 grams)

Unflavored gelatin ✕ 1 envelope (¼ ounce/7 grams)

Heavy cream ✕ 1½ cups (12 fluid ounces/ 360 milliliters)

FOR THE THYME CREAM AND PEARS:

Milk ✕ ½ cup (4 fluid ounces/120 milliliters)

Fresh thyme leaves ✕ 1 tablespoon

Egg yolks ✕ 2 large

Confectioners' sugar ✕ ⅓ cup (1¼ ounces/ 35 grams)

Chianti wine ✕ ½ cup (4 fluid ounces/ 120 milliliters)

2 small ripe pears, peeled and thinly sliced

Make the *panna cotta*: In a medium saucepan, combine the milk, cheese, and sugar and heat over medium heat, stirring constantly, until the sugar dissolves, about 5 minutes. Remove from the heat, add the gelatin, and stir until it is dissolved, then stir in the cream. Using an immersion blender or whisk, beat the mixture for 1 minute to combine the ingredients.

Pour the mixture through a fine-mesh sieve into six individual-serving ramekins or molds. Cover with plastic wrap and refrigerate until set, about 4 hours.

Make the thyme cream and pears: In a small saucepan, heat the milk and thyme over medium-high heat until warm. Remove from the heat, pour into a bowl, and let cool to room temperature. In the same saucepan, combine the egg yolks and confectioners' sugar and, using an electric mixer, beat until creamy. Pour the thyme-milk through a fine-mesh sieve into the saucepan and stir until well combined. Heat over low heat until the mixture thickens, about 4 minutes. Pour the mixture into a small bowl and cover with plastic wrap. Refrigerate until ready to use.

Combine the wine and pear slices in a small saucepan and simmer, covered, until softened. Set aside.

Run a knife around the edge of each ramekin and turn the *panna cotta* out onto a serving plate. Arrange slices of pear on one side of the plate, topped with some of the Chianti syrup. Drizzle some of the thyme cream on the *panna cotta*.

panna cotta

SERVES 8
REGION: Piedmont

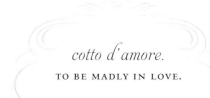

Panna cotta is a specialty of Piedmont, so I asked for help from Franco Piumatti, a professional chef from the region. His recipe creates a *panna cotta* with an ethereal mouthfeel, silky smooth, never rubbery. It provides the perfect canvas for anything that accompanies it—fresh fruit, chocolate, or caramel. Chef Franco stressed two things: One, buy the very best cream you can find at your local farmers' market and two, despite its name—"cooked cream"—do not heat the cream. Its aroma and flavor will be ruined if it's heated, so add it cold.

Milk ✕ 1½ cups (12 fluid ounces/360 milliliters)

Unflavored gelatin ✕ 1 envelope (¼ ounce/7 grams)

Sugar ✕ ⅓ cup (2¼ ounces/65 grams)

Heavy cream ✕ 2 cups (16 fluid ounces/480 milliliters)

In a medium saucepan, combine the milk, gelatin, and sugar and let stand for a minute or two so the gelatin dissolves. Bring to a low boil, stirring until the sugar and gelatin are dissolved. Remove from the heat and stir in the cream. Taste and add more sugar, if you like. Pour the mixture through a fine-mesh sieve into six individual-sized ramekins, or into a larger mold, then cover with plastic wrap and refrigerate until set, about 4 hours. To unmold, run a knife around the edge of the ramekins or mold, and turn each one out onto a serving plate. Serve cold.

UN ALTRO MODO

Coffee *Panna Cotta*: Add 1 shot freshly brewed espresso and 1 teaspoon finely ground espresso beans when you add the cream.

Hazelnut *Panna Cotta*: Add 1 tablespoon hazelnut butter (or other nut butter, such as pistachio or almond butter) when you add the sugar.

Lemon or Orange *Panna Cotta*: Add the zest of 1 lemon or ½ orange to the milk.

Drunken *Panna Cotta*: Stir in a splash of rum or your favorite liqueur when you add the sugar.

After-Eight *Panna Cotta* (*Dopo le 8*): Add fresh mint leaves to the milk, and serve topped with melted or finely chopped dark chocolate.

***Panna Cotta* with Sweet and Salty Caramel Sauce**: Top the panna cotta with this amazingly addictive caramel sauce: Simmer ½ cup (4 ounces/95 grams) sugar with ¼ cup (2 fluid ounces/60 milliliters) water in a saucepan over medium high heat until golden brown, about 8 minutes. Very slowly pour in ½ cup (4 fluid ounces/120 milliliters) cream and cook until thick, about 6 minutes. Stir in a pinch of sea salt and let cool.

licorice panna cotta

SERVES 6

REGION: Calabria

If you like licorice, even just a little, you owe it to yourself to try this recipe. It takes just a few minutes to make and you'll be rewarded with a grown-up, gourmet, creamy version of Good & Plenty.

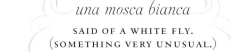

Put the licorice in a spice or coffee grinder and grind to a fine powder. You should get a little more than 2 tablespoons powder.

In a saucepan, combine 1 tablespoon of the licorice powder with the milk and sugar and bring to a low boil.

Remove from the heat and stir in the gelatin and lemon zest, stirring until the gelatin is dissolved. Stir in the cream. Taste and, if you like, add a little more licorice, reserving the rest for garnish.

Pour the mixture into six individual-serving cups or ramekins, cover with plastic wrap, and refrigerate until set, about 6 hours.

To unmold, run a knife around the edge of each ramekin and turn them out onto serving plates. Serve topped with lemon zest and a sprinkle of licorice powder.

Unsweetened licorice candies, such as Amarelli ✖ 1 ounce/30 grams

Milk ✖ 1 cup (8 fluid ounces/240 milliliters)

Sugar ✖ ½ cup (3½ ounces/100 grams)

Unflavored gelatin ✖ 1 envelope (¼ ounce/7 grams)

Grated zest of ½ lemon

Heavy cream ✖ 2½ cups (20 fluid ounces/600 milliliters)

zabaglione

SERVES 6

REGION: Piedmont, but popular throughout Italy

How three simple ingredients can produce such ecstasy is testament to the marvels of Italian cuisine. *Zabaglione* can be served warm or chilled, either by itself or with fresh berries and a slice of *pandoro* or *panettone*. I learned how to make *zabaglione* in Verona at the famed 12 Apostoli restaurant. There the chef showed me the charming way Italians measure out the ingredients using an eggshell. For every egg, he used one of the broken shells to measure the sugar and Marsala—five eggs get five half-eggshell-fulls. If you want to make more or less *zabaglione*, just increase or decrease the eggs and adjust accordingly.

val più un buon giorno con uovo, che un mal'anno con un bue.

BETTER A GOOD DAY WITH JUST AN EGG THAN A BAD YEAR FEASTING ON OX.

Egg yolks ✳ 5 large

Sugar ✳ 5 tablespoons (2¼ ounces/ 65 grams)

Marsala wine ✳ ½ cup (4 fluid ounces/ 120 milliliters)

Bring a pot of water to a boil. In a large metal or heat-proof glass bowl, combine the egg yolks and sugar and whisk until creamy. Set the bowl over the boiling water, without letting the bottom touch the water, and continue whisking. Gradually pour in the Marsala while continuing to whisk. Continue whisking until the custard has doubled in volume and is thick enough to coat a spoon, about 10 minutes. Serve warm or chilled.

barolo poached pears with chocolate sauce

Pere martine al Barolo

SERVES 4

REGION: Piedmont and Val d'Aosta

4 large pears or 8 small Martin Sech pears

Red wine, such as Barolo ✳ 3 cups (24 fluid ounces/720 milliliters)

Cloves ✳ 4 whole

Cinnamon ✳ 1 (2-inch/5-centimeter) stick

Dark brown sugar ✳ ½ cup (3½ ounces/ 100 grams)

Dark chocolate ✳ 2 ounces/55 grams

Heavy cream or milk ✳ 2 tablespoons

Peel and core the pears, but leave them whole. Put the pears, wine, cloves, cinnamon, and brown sugar in a medium saucepan and simmer over very low heat for about 30 minutes, or until the pears are tender. Remove the pears from the pan and place them on a serving plate. Continue to simmer the liquid in the pan until thick and syrupy, about 15 minutes. When ready to serve, put the chocolate and cream in a small bowl and melt the chocolate, either in a microwave oven or over a saucepan of gently simmering water. Serve the pears at room temperature, topped with wine syrup, and chocolate sauce on the side.

chocolate rice pudding

Riso nero

SERVES 8

REGION: Sicily

Rice pudding seasoned with lots of dark chocolate and hints of sweet liqueur and orange: a Sicilian classic!

In a medium saucepan, combine ½ cup (4 fluid ounces/120 milliliters) water, the milk, rice, and salt and bring to a boil. Lower the heat to low and simmer, covered, until the rice is tender, about 25 minutes. Add more milk if the mixture becomes too dry.

Remove from the heat, add the chocolate and sugar, and stir until the chocolate is dissolved. Stir in the raisins, liqueur, and pine nuts and let the mixture cool to room temperature. Serve topped with shaved chocolate and orange zest.

Milk ✕ 1½ cups (12 fluid ounces/ 360 milliliters)

Long-grain rice ✕ 1 cup (7½ ounces/ 215 grams)

Salt ✕ ¼ teaspoon

Dark chocolate ✕ 3 to 4 ounces/85 to 115 grams

Sugar ✕ ½ cup (4 ounces/95 grams)

Raisins ✕ ¾ cup (4½ ounces/130 grams)

Strega or other Italian liqueur ✕ 6 tablespoons

Pine nuts ✕ ⅓ cup (1½ ounces/40 grams)

Grated zest of 1 orange

sicilian watermelon pudding

Gelo di anguria

SERVES 4

REGION: Sicily

Watermelon juice thickened with a little cornstarch creates a light, nondairy, nonfat treat that's perfect for a hot summer day. The bits of chocolate, which whimsically mimic watermelon seeds, add nice flavor and crunch. It is often served topped with fragrant jasmine flowers.

This watermelon custard, or *gelu di miluni* in Sicilian dialect, is served all summer, but especially on July 15 in Palermo, in honor of the city's patron saint, Saint Rosalia. It's also commonly served on *Ferragosto,* August 15, Italy's national holiday that marks the start of summer vacation.

Puree the watermelon in a food processor until liquidy, and then press through a fine-mesh sieve. You will need 2 cups (16 fluid ounces/480 milliliters) liquid, so process more watermelon if necessary.

Combine the watermelon juice, cornstarch, and sugar in a saucepan and, off the heat, whisk until the cornstarch is fully dissolved. Simmer the mixture over low heat until it thickens, about 4 minutes. Remove from the heat and stir in the Maraschino liqueur. Taste and add more sugar, if you like. Pour into 4 serving cups or molds and refrigerate until firm, about 3 hours.

To serve, unmold onto serving plates or serve in the cups and garnish with chocolate and pistachios.

UN ALTRO MODO

Orange Gelo: Substitute 2 cups (16 fluid ounces/480 milliliters) freshly squeezed orange juice for the watermelon juice.

Lemon Gelo: Substitute 1 cup (8 fluid ounces/240 milliliters) freshly squeezed lemon juice diluted with 1 cup (8 fluid ounces/240 milliliters) water for the watermelon juice. Adjust the sugar to taste.

Coffee Gelo: Substitute 2 cups (16 fluid ounces/480 milliliters) freshly brewed coffee or espresso for the watermelon juice. Dilute with water and sweeten with sugar to taste.

Cinnamon Gelo: Steep several 2-inch (5-centimeter) cinnamon sticks overnight in 2 cups (16 fluid ounces/480 milliliters) water. Bring to a boil and strain, substituting this liquid for the watermelon juice.

Diced seeded watermelon ✳ 3 to 4 cups (about 1 pound/450 grams)

Cornstarch ✳ 3½ tablespoons

Sugar ✳ ⅓ cup (2¼ ounces/65 grams)

Maraschino liqueur ✳ 2 tablespoons

Dark chocolate, finely chopped

Chopped pistachios

zuppa inglese

SERVES 8 TO 10
REGION: Emilia-Romagna

This dish varies in Italy from a very creamy trifle served in a large bowl, to firmer ones, which slice like cake. This is the classic version popular in Emilia. *Savoiardi* (crisp lady fingers) are moistened with liqueur, then layered with lemon and chocolate custards and topped with meringue. A great make-ahead dessert, it's even better the next day.

    Zuppa inglese translates as English soup. But this dish is neither English nor a soup. The name may perhaps come from the word *inzuppare,* which means "to soak up," or could come from its similarity to English trifle.

FOR THE FILLINGS:

1 recipe Pastry Cream (page 197), unchilled

Grated zest and juice of 1 lemon

Dark chocolate ✳ 2½ ounces/70 grams, finely chopped

Unsweetened cocoa powder ✳ 1 tablespoon

TO ASSEMBLE:

Liqueur, such as *alchermes* (page 182), Maraschino, or Kirsch ✳ 6 tablespoons

Warm water ✳ ⅓ cup (2½ fluid ounces/ 70 milliliters)

Sugar ✳ 4 tablespoons (1¾ ounces/ 50 grams)

Savoiardi (crisp ladyfingers) ✳ 48 cookies (one 14-ounce/400-gram package)

Egg whites ✳ 3 large

Confectioners' sugar ✳ ⅞ cup (3 ounces/ 85 grams)

Cherries, either fresh, frozen, or in brandy

Make the fillings: Pour half of the hot pastry cream (about 3 cups, or 24 fluid ounces/720 milliliters) into a medium bowl and stir in the lemon zest and juice. Pour the remaining pastry cream into another medium bowl and stir in the chocolate and cocoa powder until the chocolate is melted.

Cover both bowls with plastic wrap, with the wrap touching the surface of the custards so they don't form skins, and refrigerate until cold, at least 4 hours.

To assemble the dessert: In a small bowl, combine the liqueur, warm water, and sugar to taste and stir until the sugar is dissolved.

Arrange one layer of *savoiardi* on an oven-safe serving platter or bowl and, brush with half of the liqueur mixture, then spread with the lemon custard. Place a second layer of *savoiardi* on top and brush with the remaining liqueur syrup. Spread with the chocolate custard. Cover with plastic wrap and refrigerate the *zuppa inglese* overnight or for up to 24 hours.

Just before serving, preheat the broiler.

In a large bowl, with an electric mixer, beat the egg whites and confectioners' sugar until glossy and stiff. Remove the plastic wrap from the *zuppa inglese* and top with cherries. Spread with the meringue and put the cake on the lowest rack of the oven, away from the broiler. Broil until the meringue sets and becomes firm, about 5 minutes. Serve immediately.

coffee on a fork

Caffè in forchetta

SERVES 6

REGION: Valle d'Aosta and northern Italy

Coffee and dessert in one! This is a silky custard that forms a crunchy caramel top crust as it bakes.

Preheat the oven to 350°F (180°C). Add boiling water to a large roasting pan until one-third full. Place 6 ramekins or oven-safe coffee cups in the pan.

In a large bowl, with a whisk or an electric mixer, beat the eggs, egg yolks, and sugar to taste until creamy. Add the milk and espresso and beat until well blended. Do not overbeat, or the mixture will become too frothy. If that happens, just allow it to settle for 30 minutes or pour the mixture through a fine-mesh sieve.

Pour into the ramekins and bake for 30 minutes, until a golden crust forms on top. It will be a little jiggly in the center. That's normal; it will firm up as it cools. Remove the pan from the oven and the ramekins from the pan. Let cool to room temperature, then refrigerate until ready to serve. Serve cold.

Eggs ✕ 5 large

Egg yolks ✕ 2 large

Sugar ✕ 1 cup (7 ounces/200 grams)

Milk ✕ 1½ cups (12 fluid ounces/ 360 milliliters)

Freshly brewed espresso, cold ✕ ¾ cup (6 fluid ounces/180 milliliters—about 3 shots)

monte bianco

REGION: Piedmont, Valle d'Aosta, and northern Italy

Chocolate-chestnut puree topped with brandy-spiked whipped cream—a melt-in-your-mouth delight. Called *monte bianco,* or white mountain, because the dessert looks like the snow-capped Alps, many Italians elaborate on the theme and scatter candied violets and crushed candied chestnuts on the "mountain" to look like flowers and rocks.

Fresh chestnuts (see Note) ✕ 1 pound/
455 grams

Milk ✕ 2½ cups (20 fluid ounces/
600 milliliters)

Sugar ✕ ¾ cup (5¼ ounces/150 grams)

Fennel seeds ✕ 2 tablespoons

Dark chocolate ✕ 2 ounces/55 grams,
finely chopped

Brandy or rum ✕ ¼ cup plus 1 tablespoon
(2½ fluid ounces/75 milliliters)

Pure vanilla extract ✕ 1 teaspoon

Heavy cream ✕ 1 cup (8 fluid ounces/
240 milliliters)

Pierce the skin of each chestnut with a knife. Boil them in a large pot of water until tender, about 20 minutes. Drain and let cool only slightly—it's much easier to peel them while they're warm. Peel the chestnuts and set aside.

In a medium saucepan, combine the milk, ½ cup (3.5 ounces/95 grams) of the sugar, and fennel and cook over low heat to release the fennel's flavor, about 5 minutes. Strain to remove the fennel and return the liquid to the saucepan. Add the chestnuts and simmer for 20 minutes. Put the warm chestnut mixture into a food processor along with the chocolate, ¼ cup (2 fluid ounces/60 milliliters) of the brandy, and the vanilla. Pulse to combine, then process until very smooth. Let cool to room temperature, then cover with plastic wrap and refrigerate for at least 1 hour or up to 2 days.

Put a tall glass upside down in the center of a serving plate. Press the chestnut mixture through a potato ricer and form it into a mountain-shaped cone around the glass. Remove the glass.

In a large bowl, with an electric mixer, whip the cream and remaining ¼ cup (1¾ ounces/50 grams) of the remaining sugar until firm peaks form. Stir in the remaining 1 tablespoon brandy. Fill the hollow left by the glass with whipped cream and top the chestnut "mountain" with more whipped cream. Serve immediately.

NOTE: You can also make this dessert with ready-roasted chestnuts, available in most supermarkets, or with dried chestnuts, my personal favorite. The dried ones are great because the flavor is a little more intense than the ready-roasted jarred variety. Just soak the dried chestnuts overnight, then simmer in water until soft.

ricotta "sundae"

Ricotta condita

SERVES AS MANY AS YOU LIKE

REGION: Lazio and southern Italy

In Italy, where locally made fresh ricotta is a matter of town pride, it's often served for dessert, accompanied by an assortment of toppings—just like our ice-cream sundaes. In Rome, the favorite topping is finely ground espresso beans, sugar, and a splash of rum. In other regions, the topping of choice may be grated dark chocolate, honey, or fruit preserves. This is an effortless and fun dessert.

Give each guest a small bowlful of the ricotta. Serve accompanied by the other ingredients, to taste.

UN ALTRO MODO

Sweet Saffron Ricotta: Add a few drops of hot water to a pinch or two of saffron threads to release the color and flavor. Blend the saffron into ricotta, sweetened with sugar and Marsala wine.

Rum and Chocolate Ricotta: Using a fork, combine 16 ounces/ 455 grams ricotta with ½ cup (3½ ounces/100 grams) sugar, 2 ounces (55 grams) grated dark chocolate, and 3 tablespoons golden raisins that were soaked in ⅓ cup (2½ fluid ounces/75 milliliters) rum until plump. Refrigerate for a few hours for the flavors to meld. Serve at room temperature.

Ricotta cheese

Finely ground espresso beans

Superfine sugar

Rum, amaretto, or other Italian liqueur

Dark chocolate, grated on a cheese grater

Ground cinnamon

Fruit preserves

Fresh fruit

Honey

cantucci-caramel custard

Budino di cantucci

SERVES 8

REGION: Tuscany

This is like flan or crème caramel, but with Italian flare. A foolproof custard that comes together with a few kitchen staples plus *cantucci*, almond biscotti from Tuscany. I'm grateful to Ubaldo Corsini, the charming owner of Corsini Biscotti in Tuscany, for teaching me to make this pretty dessert that makes such good use of his fabulous *cantucci*.

Sugar ✳ 1 cup (7 ounces/200 grams)

Eggs ✳ 3 large

Egg yolks ✳ 2 large

Pure vanilla extract ✳ 1 tablespoon

Milk ✳ 1¼ cups (10 fluid ounces/300 milliliters)

Heavy cream ✳ 1¼ cups (10 fluid ounces/300 milliliters)

Cantucci cookies (almond biscotti) ✳ 4 ounces/115 grams

Preheat the oven to 350°F (180°C). Put eight individual-serving ramekins (see Note) in a deep roasting pan filled with 2 inches (5 centimeters) of hot water.

Put ½ cup (3½ ounces/100 grams) of the sugar in a small, heavy saucepan and sprinkle with ½ teaspoon water. Cook, stirring with a wooden spoon, over medium heat until the sugar melts and becomes golden , about 5 minutes. Carefully divide the mixture among the ramekins so that it covers the bottom. Set aside.

In a large bowl, using an electric mixer or whisk, beat the remaining sugar, eggs, egg yolks, and vanilla until light yellow and creamy.

Meanwhile, in a medium saucepan, heat the milk and cream until bubbles just begin to form around the edges of the pan, then slowly pour the hot milk mixture into the egg mixture and gently whisk to combine. Stir in the cookie pieces. Using a large spoon or ladle, divide the mixture among the ramekins, being sure to distribute the cookie pieces evenly. Bake for about 45 minutes, until firm and light golden on top. Remove the ramekins from the pan and let cool to room temperature, then refrigerate until ready to serve. To serve, run a knife around the edges of the ramekins and turn out onto serving plates so the caramel is on top. Serve cold.

NOTE: You can also make this dessert in a loaf pan. It will just need an extra 5 minutes in the oven.

amaretti custard

Bonet di amaretti

SERVES 8 TO 10

REGION: Piedmont

Creamy custard topped with simple-to-make caramel—this is a fool-proof classic that looks and tastes impressive. Master this basic Italian recipe, which is a snap, and you can create hundreds of variations.

The name *bonet* comes from the Piedmont dialect for "little cap," referring to the hat-shaped cooking containers it was made in. Many people in Piedmont, however, will tell you that the name comes from the fact that this dessert was the last thing eaten at a meal, just as a hat is the last thing you put on when you're ready to leave.

Sugar ✳ 1 cup (7 ounces/200 grams)

Milk ✳ 2 cups (16 fluid ounces/480 milliliters)

Amaretti (crisp almond cookies) ✳ 3 ounces/85 grams (about 20 cookies)

Unsweetened cocoa powder ✳ 2 tablespoons

Eggs ✳ 4 large

Egg yolks ✳ 2 large

Rum ✳ 3 tablespoons

Freshly brewed hot espresso ✳ 2 tablespoons

Preheat the oven to 350°F (180°C). In a medium saucepan, combine ½ cup (3½ ounces/100 grams) of the sugar and ½ cup (4 fluid ounces/120 milliliters) water and boil until the mixture becomes a golden caramel color. Let the syrup cool for a few minutes, then pour into a medium (5-by-9-inch/12-by-23-centimeter) loaf pan. Chill the pan in the refrigerator to harden the syrup.

Meanwhile, put the milk in the saucepan you just used to make the sugar syrup. Bring the milk to a low boil over medium heat. Remove from the heat and set aside.

In a food processor, combine the *amaretti*, the remaining ½ cup (3½ ounces/100 grams) sugar, and the cocoa powder and pulse until the *amaretti* are finely ground. Add the eggs, egg yolks, rum, and espresso and process until combined. Very gradually process in the warm milk. Process until well combined.

Pour the mixture into the prepared loaf pan. Put the loaf pan in a larger roasting pan filled halfway with hot water. Bake until set, about 50 minutes. The custard will be slightly soft in the middle, but will solidify as it cools. Refrigerate until cold.

Turn the cold *bonet* onto a serving platter so the pretty caramel bottom is on top. Slice and serve.

UN ALTRO MODO

Citrus Bonet: Omit the cocoa powder and espresso and add the juice and grated zest of 1 lemon or ½ orange.

Nut Bonet: Omit the cocoa and espresso and add a handful of finely crushed nuts, such as pistachios or almonds.

traditional tiramisù

SERVES 6

REGION: Veneto originally, but now popular throughout Italy

Tiramisù appears on just about every restaurant menu in every region of Italy, but it's a favorite of Italian home cooks as well. First created in the 1960s in a restaurant in the town of Treviso, close to Venice, tiramisù means "pick me up" in Italian. Urban legend has it that a very nice brothel near the restaurant served it to their lovely "employees" between shifts.

This is the classic version. Store-bought *savoiardi* are dipped in coffee and layered with whipped mascarpone cheese, then topped with grated chocolate or cocoa powder.

In a medium bowl, beat the egg whites and 1 tablespoon of the sugar until soft peaks form.

In another medium bowl, beat the egg yolks and the remaining 4 tablespoons sugar until creamy and pale yellow. Beat in the mascarpone and then gently fold in the whites.

Dip 6 *savoiardi* in the espresso spiked with a splash of rum and use them to line the bottom of a high-rimmed serving dish. Spread one third of the mascarpone mixture over the *savoiardi*. Repeat to make another two layers.

Top the final mascarpone layer with a generous amount of grated chocolate or cocoa powder just before serving.

UN ALTRO MODO

Fruit Tiramisù: Instead of coffee, dip the *savoiardi* into diluted jam or sweet liqueur, and layer with fresh fruit in addition to the mascarpone mixture. Top with shaved white chocolate.

Eggs ✕ 3 large, separated

Sugar ✕ 5 tablespoons (2¼ ounces/ 65 grams)

Mascarpone cheese about ✕ 1½ cups (12 ounces/340 grams)

Savoiardi (crisp ladyfingers) ✕ 20 cookies

Brewed espresso ✕ 1 cup (8 fluid ounces/ 240 milliliters)

Rum

Dark chocolate, finely grated; or unsweetened cocoa powder

ognuno tira l'acqua al suo mulino.

EVERYONE DRAWS WATER TO HIS OWN MILL. (EVERYONE ACTS IN HIS OWN INTEREST.)

updated tiramisù

MAKES 6 AVERAGE OR 12 SMALL PORTIONS

REGION: Throughout Italy

meglio un uovo oggi che una gallina domani.

BETTER AN EGG TODAY THAN A CHICKEN TOMORROW. (A BIRD IN THE HAND IS WORTH TWO IN THE BUSH.)

Tiramisù is traditionally made with raw eggs, so my curiosity was piqued when in Le Tre Zucche, a Rome restaurant, my waitress, listing the desserts, mentioned tiramisù "for pregnant women," explaining that it was made without the usual raw eggs or rum. It was offered in mini or large, and not being sure if I'd like it, I went with the small size. What arrived was an espresso cup with lush, cool mascarpone custard that contrasted wonderfully with the layer of warm espresso-moistened *savoiardi* at the bottom of the cup. One bite was all it took for me to be certain of two things: One, I deeply regretted having ordered the mini, and two, if necessary I would literally beg the chef to teach me how to make it so I could include it in this cookbook.

Not only is his tiramisù just as delicious as the traditional version, but his technique of whipping the eggs with hot sugar syrup means there are no raw eggs to worry about, and also the custard stays light and fluffy for up to 2 days in the fridge. This is a perfect make-ahead dessert that you can serve in mini portions in espresso cups, or normal-sized portions in dessert bowls or coffee cups.

Egg yolks ✴ 5 large

Sugar ✴ ½ cup (3½ ounces/100 grams)

Mascarpone cheese ✴ 1 cup (8 ounces/225 grams)

Heavy cream ✴ ¼ cup (2 fluid ounces/60 milliliters)

Savoiardi (crisp ladyfingers) ✴ 12 cookies

Freshly brewed hot espresso or coffee ✴ 1 cup (8 fluid ounces/240 milliliters)

Rum (optional)

Unsweetened cocoa powder

Put the egg yolks in the bowl of an electric stand mixer fitted with the whisk attachment and beat on the highest setting until light yellow and fluffy, at least 5 minutes.

Meanwhile, heat the sugar and ¼ cup (2 fluid ounces/60 milliliters) water in a small saucepan until the syrup bubbles and reaches 250°F (120°C) on a candy thermometer. With the mixer still on its highest setting, slowly pour the hot syrup into the egg yolks and continue beating for 15 minutes. (It's important to whisk them for this long so that the mixture stays fluffy when you add the next ingredients.) Add the mascarpone and cream and beat on medium speed just until combined, about 20 seconds. You can keep this custard, covered with plastic wrap, in the refrigerator for up to 2 days.

Brew the espresso or coffee. Break 1 *savoiardi* into each espresso cup, or 2 into each coffee mug or dessert bowl. Pour the espresso over the *savoiardi* so they are fully moistened and, if you like, add a splash of rum. Top with a generous dollop or two of the mascarpone mixture. Dust with cocoa powder. Serve immediately.

NOTE: For a two-tone effect, dust half the surface of the tiramisù with cocoa powder and the other half with *savoiardi* crumbs.

CHAPTER SEVEN

weird and wonderful, unique and unusual desserts

DOLCI PARTICOLARI

"peaches"

Pesche dolci

MAKES ABOUT 40

REGION: Abruzzo and Molise

To make these kitschy-chic faux peaches, two rounded cookies are joined together with a creamy filling, then dipped in red-tinted liqueur and rolled in sugar. They look just like small, fuzzy peaches. The cookies absorb the filling and the liqueur, and acquire the moist, dense texture of summer-ripe fruit. There's even a faux peach pit in the center—a whole almond—the final touch to this culinary *trompe l'oeil*. A real show-stopper and indescribably delicious!

Make the cookies: Preheat the oven to 350°F (180°C). Line two large baking sheets with parchment paper.

Sift the flour and sugar together onto a work surface and make a well in the center. Add the eggs, butter, milk, vanilla, and baking powder to the well and slowly mix in the flour until a dough forms. Knead until well combined.

Pinch off a small portion of the dough and roll it into a small ball, about 1 inch (2.5 centimeters) in diameter. Press the ball onto the prepared baking sheet so it is flattened to a half dome. Repeat with the remaining dough. Each ball will become half of the peach. Continue until all the dough is used up. Bake for about 25 minutes, until light golden.

While still warm, scrape out a wide hollow in the flat side of each ball with a espresso spoon or tip of a knife.

Assemble the "peaches": Put the *alchermes*, diluted with ¼ cup (2 fluid ounces/60 milliliters) water, in a small bowl. Put some sugar on a small plate.

Divide the hollowed-out cookies into pairs of roughly the same size. Take a pair and fill the hollow side of each cookie with lots of pastry cream. Put an almond in the center of one of the cookies and gently press them together. Some of the cream will ooze out. That's normal.

Slowly roll each "peach" in the liqueur, then in the sugar. Put the "peaches" on a platter, cover with plastic wrap, and refrigerate for at least 12 hours, or up to 36, before serving. This is an important step, as they need time in the refrigerator to absorb the pastry cream and soften.

FOR THE COOKIES:

All-purpose flour ✖ 4 cups (16 ounces/455 grams)

Sugar ✖ 1 cup (7 ounces/200 grams)

Eggs ✖ 2 large

Butter ✖ 6 tablespoons (3 ounces/85 grams)

Milk ✖ ⅓ cup (2½ fluid ounces/75 milliliters)

Pure vanilla extract ✖ 2 teaspoons

Baking powder ✖ 2 teaspoons

TO FILL AND ASSEMBLE:

Alchermes (page 182) or Kirsch tinted red with food coloring ✖ ¼ cup (2 fluid ounces/60 milliliters)

Sugar

Pastry Cream (page 197), lemon curd, or vanilla pudding ✖ 1½ cups (12 fluid ounces/360 milliliters)

40 whole almonds

sweet chickpea baked ravioli

gnocchi, rape, fave,
e ceci: due ti saziano per dieci.

GNOCCHI, TURNIPS, BEANS, AND
CHICKPEAS: TWO FILL YOU UP FOR TEN
HOURS. (SAID OF VERY FILLING FOODS.)

Panzarotti con ceci

MAKES ABOUT 4 DOZEN

REGION: Puglia

These ravioli are baked, not boiled, creating irresistible crisp bundles filled with mashed chickpeas and jam. Chickpeas aren't a typical dessert ingredient, but they sure should be! Pureed, they are velvety on the tongue and add a pleasing denseness.

    Panzerotti, in Puglia dialect, means "tummy," referring to the little pouch in the center of the ravioli.

FOR THE FILLING:

Cooked chickpeas ✖ 1½ cups (8 ounces/225 grams)

Cherry jam ✖ 1 cup (8 fluid ounces/240 milliliters)

Liqueur, such as amaretto, limoncello, or mandarino ✖ 2 to 4 tablespoons

Grated zest of ½ lemon

Honey or sugar to taste

Ground cinnamon to taste

Egg ✖ 1 large

FOR THE DOUGH:

All-purpose flour ✖ 3½ cups (16 ounces/455 grams)

Sugar ✖ ½ cup (3½ ounces/100 grams)

Salt ✖ ¼ teaspoon

Olive oil ✖ 2 tablespoons

White wine ✖ ½ cup (4 fluid ounces/120 milliliters)

Warm water

Confectioners' sugar, honey, *mosto cotto,* or *vin cotto*

Make the filling: Pass the chickpeas through a food mill until you get a nice thick, smooth paste. Stir in the jam and liqueur to taste. Stir in the lemon zest and cinnamon to taste, then add sugar or honey, if you like. When you have tasted it and are happy with the flavor, mix in the egg. You can make the filling several days ahead. Refrigerate until ready to use.

Make the dough: Sift the flour, granulated sugar, and salt onto a work surface and make a well in the center. Pour the oil and wine into the well and incorporate the flour, a little at a time, until a dough forms. Add warm water, a little at a time, if the dough feels tough. Knead the dough until smooth. Put in a resealable plastic bag or wrap in plastic wrap.

Preheat the oven to 350°F (180°C). Line two or three baking sheets with parchment paper. Put a large, clean cotton cloth on a work surface for assembling and cutting the ravioli (see Note).

Leaving the rest covered, take a small portion of the dough (about one eighth of it) and either pass it through a pasta machine (#3 hole size, not thinner) or use a rolling pin to roll the dough out into a 3- to 4-inch-wide (7.5- to 10-centimeter-wide) strip of dough. Repeat to make another strip. Make just 2 strips at a time, so you can fill and cut the ravioli without the rest of the dough getting dry. Put a strip of dough on the cloth and drop tablespoon-size mounds of the filling onto the dough about 1½ inches (4 centimeters) apart. Top with the second strip of dough. Using your fingers, press the top layer of dough around the filling; using a ravioli cutter, cut out square-shaped ravioli. Repeat with the remaining dough and filling.

Put the ravioli on the baking sheets and bake, in batches, for about 25 minutes, until golden. Serve warm, sprinkled with confectioners' sugar, or serve cold, dipped in honey or sweet wine.

NOTE: I learned a fabulous tip from Franca Artuso, the seventy-two-year-old grandmother from Basilicata who taught me this recipe. Instead of using a bunch of flour on the work surface to keep the dough from sticking, spread out a yard or so of clean white cotton canvas cloth, available at fabric stores. It works miracles. The dough doesn't stick or dry out from the extra flour. Plus—and this is a big deal for me—cleanup is much easier. No little stuck-on bits of flour all over the place. Just toss the cloth in the washing machine when you're done and enjoy dessert!

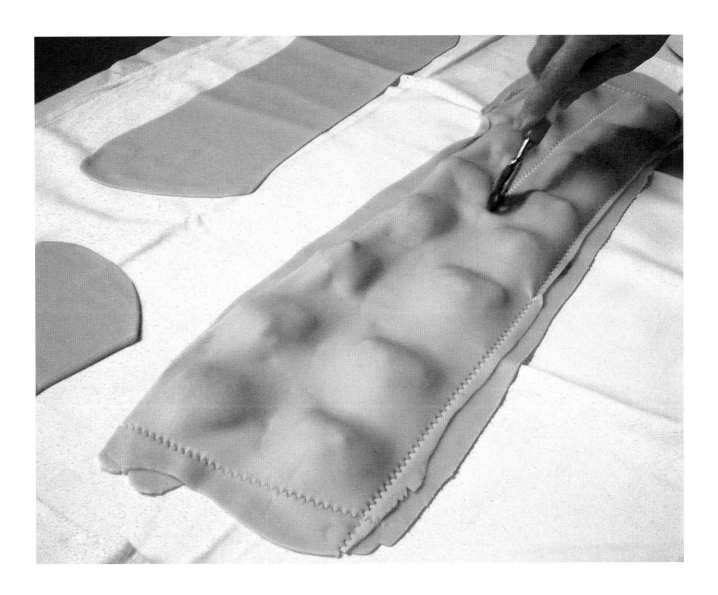

sicilian pasta crisps

Pasta fritta alla Siracusa

SERVES 6

REGION: Sicily

Twirled forkfuls of honey-sweetened angel hair pasta—crunchy on the edges and soft in the center—are scrumptious and a snap to prepare. If you're skeptical about pasta for dessert, do a little taste-test. The next time you cook a pot of spaghetti, save a little and try it. I guarantee you'll boil up a bigger pot next time, if not right then and there.

Angel hair or vermicelli pasta ✖ ⅓ pound/150 grams

Salt

Honey ✖ ¼ cup (2 fluid ounces/60 milliliters)

Finely minced candied orange peel ✖ 2 tablespoons

Sunflower or other vegetable oil

Pistachios, very finely crushed

Ground cinnamon

Cook the pasta in salted water according to the package directions. Drain.

Meanwhile, in a small bowl, combine the honey and candied orange peel.

Put about ¼ inch (6 millimeters) of oil in a small frying pan and heat until hot but not smoking. Twirl small forkfuls of the pasta, drop them into the hot oil, and cook until golden and crisp at the edges. Turn and cook on the other side for just a few seconds. Drain the pasta crisps on a plate lined with paper towels. Arrange the pasta crisps on a serving plate. Serve warm, drizzled with the honey mixture and topped with a sprinkle of pistachios and cinnamon.

hazelnut chocolate pasta

Pasta al gianduiotti

SERVES 4

REGION: Piedmont

I love pasta. I love it in any shape, any length, and with any sauce. I also love chocolate, so I was thrilled to discover that Italians combine the two! All of Italy's many pasta dessert recipes enchant me, but this is a standout because it showcases my favorite Italian candy—*gianduiotti,* creamy hazelnut chocolates. *Gianduiotti* are tossed with hot pasta, creating a rich, silky sauce, which pops with roasted hazelnut flavor. It's wonderful plain but, if you like, you can dress it up with a splash of hazelnut liqueur, a sprinkle of crushed hazelnuts, and a dollop of whipped cream.

Angel hair or other thin long pasta ✄
8 ounces/225 grams

12 *gianduiotti* (hazelnut chocolates) or hazelnut chocolate ✄ ¾ cup
(6 fluid ounces/180 milliliters)

Whipped cream or mascarpone cheese, chopped hazelnuts, and hazelnut liqueur such as Frangelico, optional

Cook the pasta in water according to the package directions. Drain.

Put 1 *gianduiotti* in each of 4 wineglasses or dessert bowls. Divide the hot pasta among them and top each with 2 more *gianduiotti.*

Top each serving with a dollop of whipped cream, a splash of liqueur, and sprinkle of hazelnuts, if you like. Serve immediately.

in italy

Back in the Renaissance, pasta was a luxury food, reserved for the rich and for special occasions. It was often served topped with other luxury foods like sugar and cinnamon.

Today throughout Italy many sweet pasta and lasagna dishes remain popular. Some are served as first courses, especially at Christmastime, but others are served as desserts.

— Almond Spaghetti (*spaghetti latte di mandorle*): In Puglia, homemade spaghetti is boiled in rich almond milk instead of water and then served topped with sugar and cinnamon.

— Christmas Walnut Macaroni (*maccheroni natalizi con le noci;* page 161) is a specialty of Lazio, often served on Christmas Eve.

— *Lasagne al forno,* popular in the Veneto region, is lasagna layered with fresh sliced apples, dried figs, walnuts, raisins, and poppy seeds.

gianduia chocolate: italy's favorite flavor

According to Clara Vada Padovani, acclaimed Italian food historian, Italian chocolate expert, and co-author of *Gianduiotto Mania,* "The marriage between hazelnuts and chocolate was made in Italy, in Turin, during the mid-1800s, when, because of the Napoleonic Wars, transport of goods, like cocoa beans, was blocked between America and Europe. *Oro bruno,* brown gold, as they called cocoa powder, had become scarce so Piedmont chocolate makers began to use hazelnuts, which were plentiful in that region, to extend their meager supplies. The result was a creamy, flavorful delight that became an instant success. In 1867, this new chocolate flavor was christened Gianduia, after a fictitious Turin Carnival character that loves good food and wine. The chocolate was formed into small candies, wrapped in paper, and given out at the Carnival in Turin. It's important to note that this was the very first time ever that chocolate candy was individually wrapped in paper!"

Today in Italy, all *gianduiotto*—no matter the maker—come wrapped in foil. "In 2001 the Codex Alimentarius Commission of the World Trade Organization established *gianduia* as the fourth category of chocolate, after milk, dark and white chocolates. Authentic *gianduiotto,* small *gianduia* chocolate candies, must each weigh no more than .4 ounces (12 grams), be shaped like an upside-down canoe, and have a pronounced aroma of toasted hazelnuts," stresses Clara Vada Padovani.

yogurt semifreddo with radicchio marmalade

Semifreddo con radicchio e yogurt

SERVES 6
REGION: Veneto

Many pastry chefs from the Treviso area have been inspired to create a variety of desserts using the region's famed *radicchio di Treviso*. This one is my favorite. Radicchio is transformed into an exquisite marmalade and added to yogurt to create an exceptional *semifreddo*. I've remade this recipe, even without the radicchio, dozens of times. It's a terrific basic. I really love the fact that with just a container of yogurt and some gelatin I can create a quick and healthy dessert. Substitute other flavors of marmalades or make it without, topped with fresh fruit, chocolate sauce, or a drizzle of honey.

Make the marmalade: Cut the radicchio into very thin strips, then mince the strips. Bring 1 cup (8 fluid ounces/240 milliliters) water to a boil in a medium saucepan, stir in the radicchio, and simmer for 1 minute. Drain the water.

Add the butter and sugar to the radicchio, stir to combine, and cook, stirring occasionally, until very soft, at least 30 minutes. Remove from the heat and stir in the lemon zest, liqueur, and grappa. Set aside.

Make the *semifreddo*: Put the gelatin in a bowl and stir in the boiling water. Stir until the gelatin is dissolved, then stir in most of the marmalade until well combined, reserving the rest of the marmalade for garnish. Let cool to room temperature, then stir in the yogurt until creamy and well combined.

Divide the mixture among six single-serving ramekins or in one larger mold, cover with plastic wrap, and refrigerate until firm, about 3 hours.

Unmold the *semifreddo* onto serving plates or a platter, drizzle with honey, and garnish with the reserved marmalade.

FOR THE MARMALADE:

Radicchio, preferably radicchio Variegato Castelfranco or radicchio di Treviso ✖ 8 ounces/225 grams

Butter ✖ 1 tablespoon

Sugar ✖ ½ cup (3½ ounces/100 grams)

Grated zest of ½ lemon

Sweet liqueur, such as amaretto ✖ 2 tablespoons

Grappa ✖ 2 tablespoons

FOR THE SEMIFREDDO:

Unflavored gelatin ✖ 1 envelope (¼ ounce/ 7 grams)

Boiling water ✖ 1 cup (8 fluid ounces/ 240 milliliters)

Plain European-style thick yogurt ✖ 16 ounces/455 grams

Chestnut honey ✖ ½ cup (4 fluid ounces/ 120 milliliters), warmed

tuscany's sweet spinach pie

Torta co' bischeri agli spinaci

SERVES 8 TO 10

REGION: Tuscany

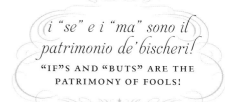
The ground almond–spinach filling is light and satisfyingly spongy—almost soufflélike. As with zucchini bread and carrot cake, the spinach contributes an earthy undertone, moistness, and an unusually brilliant color.

In Italian, *bischeri* is the name for the tuning frets on stringed instruments, and the pie crust is shaped with thick pinches of dough that mimic their shape.

Lots of chefs and food bloggers helped me wrap my head around this strange but delicious dessert. Blogger Pinella Orgiana really went all out to ensure that I got it right. Pinella made it in Italy at the same time I was making it here in the States, and she sent me step-by-step photos via e-mail as we both worked. The lovely photo on the right is hers.

FOR THE CRUST:

00 flour ✖ 4 cups (18 ounces/510 grams)

Butter ✖ 18 tablespoons (9 ounces/ 255 grams)

Sugar ✖ 7/8 cup (6 ounces/170 grams)

Egg yolks ✖ 4 large

Baking powder ✖ 2 teaspoons

Grated zest of 1 lemon

Salt ✖ 1/4 teaspoon

Make the crust: In a large bowl, in a food processor, or on a work surface, combine the flour, butter, and sugar until the mixture resembles coarse sand. Add the egg yolks, baking powder, lemon zest, and salt and mix until a dough forms. Shape the dough into a disk, cover with plastic wrap, and refrigerate for at least 30 minutes.

Lightly butter a 10-inch (25-centimeter) deep-dish pie pan.

Roll two thirds of the dough out into a circle large enough to line the pan and hang well over the sides. If you like, make a series of "fret" shapes along the outer edge of the dough. To do that, fold the edges of dough over, and cut into the edges and gently press "fret" shapes by pinching the dough between thumb and forefinger at a distance of about 1/2 inch (12 millimeters) apart. With a fork, pierce the bottom and sides of the crust all over.

Roll the remaining dough out into a circle and cut into strips to form lattices over the top of the filling. Refrigerate all the dough, covered in plastic wrap, until ready to use.

Make the filling: Cook the spinach in a few tablespoons of salted water until tender. Let cool to room temperature. Squeeze out all the excess water, then finely chop the spinach in a mini food processor. Set aside.

In a food processor, grind the almonds until the texture resembles coarse sand. Set aside.

In a large bowl, beat the egg yolks with ⅓ cup (2¼ ounces/65 grams) of the granulated sugar until creamy and light yellow. Add the almonds and beat until well combined. Add the spinach, candied peel, and liqueur and stir until well combined.

In a separate large bowl, beat the egg whites until soft peaks form, then add the remaining ⅓ cup (2¼ ounces/65 grams) granulated sugar and beat until stiff, glossy peaks form.

Slowly fold the whites into the egg yolk mixture. Pour into the bottom piecrust. Sprinkle with the pine nuts and top with the dough strips in a lattice pattern. Bake for about 1 hour, until golden.

Cool to room temperature on a wire rack, then sprinkle with confectioners' sugar and serve.

FOR THE FILLING:

Frozen spinach ✖ 12 ounces/340 grams

Salt

Blanched whole almonds ✖ 1½ cups (8 ounces/225 grams)

Eggs ✖ 4 large, separated

Sugar ✖ ⅔ cup (4½ ounces/130 grams)

A small handful minced candied citron or lemon peel

Marschino or other liqueur ✖ 4 tablespoons

Pine nuts ✖ 2 tablespoons

Confectioners' sugar

chocolate eggplant

Melanzane al cioccolato

SERVES 6

REGION: Campania, especially the Amalfi coast

Yes, you read that right. Chocolate eggplant. Layers of eggplant are spread with ricotta and chocolate, then refrigerated and served icy cold. The eggplant plays nicely against the sweet filling and dark chocolate sauce.

Melanzane al cioccolato is prepared in dozens of ways along the Amalfi coast. Although it's traditionally fried, more and more Italian chefs and home cooks are making lighter versions by baking, broiling, grilling, or even poaching the eggplant.

Eggplants ✳ 3 to 4 small

Salt

Flour, for dredging

Olive oil

Heavy cream ✳ 1 cup (8 fluid ounces/ 240 milliliters)

Dark chocolate ✳ 8 ounces/225 grams, chopped

Sweet liqueur such as amaretto or limoncello

Ricotta cheese ✳ 16 ounces/455 grams

Sugar ✳ ¼ cup (1¾ ounces/50 grams)

Amaretti (crisp almond cookies) ✳ 6 cookies, crushed

Sliced almonds ✳ ¼ cup (1 ounce/30 grams)

Minced candied orange peel ✳ 2 tablespoons

Candied cherries and other candied fruit

Peel and slice the eggplants lengthwise about ½ inch (12 millimeters) thick. Sprinkle lightly with salt.

Lightly dredge the eggplant slices in flour. Heat ¼ inch of oil in a medium skillet until hot but not smoking and fry the eggplant in batches until golden on both sides. Drain on a paper towel–lined plate and blot both sides to remove any excess oil. Repeat until all the eggplant slices have been cooked. Set aside.

Put the cream in a small saucepan and heat over medium-high heat, until bubbles just begin to form at the edge of the pan. Do not boil. Remove from the heat and stir in the chocolate until it is melted. Add a splash of liqueur and stir to combine. Taste and add sugar and more liqueur, if you like. Set the chocolate sauce aside.

In a large bowl, with a whisk or fork, beat the ricotta and sugar together until smooth and creamy. Stir in the *amaretti*, almonds, and candied orange peel until well blended. Taste and add more sugar, if you like.

Assemble the dessert as you would lasagna: Arrange one layer of eggplant in the bottom of a high-rimmed serving platter or in a baking pan. Spread one third of the ricotta filling over the eggplant slices, and top with a drizzle of the chocolate sauce.

Repeat to make 2 more layers. Finish the dessert by topping with a fourth and final layer of eggplant and any remaining chocolate sauce and a sprinkle of sliced almonds. Garnish with candied fruit, if you like. (Alternatively, create individual portions using one eggplant as seen in the photo at right.)

Cover with plastic wrap and refrigerate until the ricotta sets and the dessert is cold, about 2 hours. Serve cold.

radicchio almond carrot cake

Torta ciosota

SERVES 8 TO 10

REGION: Veneto

occhio malocchio prezzemolo e finocchio.

EYE, EVIL EYE, PARSLEY AND FENNEL. (A RHYME SAID TO KEEP AWAY BAD LUCK.)

With the surprise addition of bittersweet radicchio, this vibrant red-and-orange-speckled cake becomes sophisticated comfort food. I'm indebted to Michele Organte, a superb chef from the Veneto, who helped me experiment with dozens of radicchio dessert recipes from the region. In the end, I chose this Veneto favorite, which is amazingly moist and full of flavor, that was taught to him by his grandmother.

Butter ✷ 8 tablespoons (4 ounces/ 115 grams), melted

00 flour ✷ 1¾ cups (7 ounces/200 grams)

Eggs ✷ 3 large

Sugar ✷ 1 cup (7 ounces/200 grams)

Almond flour ✷ 1 cup (3½ ounces/ 100 grams)

Carrots ✷ 3 small (7 ounces/200 grams total), grated

Radicchio ✷ ¾ small round head, finely minced

Baking powder ✷ 2 teaspoons

Salt ✷ ¼ teaspoon

Pinch of ground cinnamon

Confectioners' sugar

Preheat the oven to 350°F (180°C). Butter and flour an 8½-inch (21.5-centimeter) round cake pan.

In a large bowl, with an electric mixer, beat the eggs and sugar together until light yellow and creamy. Beat in the 00 and almond flours until combined. With a wooden spoon, stir in the carrots, radicchio, butter, baking powder, salt, and cinnamon and mix until well combined.

Pour into the prepared pan and bake for 30 to 35 minutes, until golden and a toothpick inserted in the center comes out clean. Cool to room temperature on a wire rack, then turn out of the pan. Sprinkle with confectioners' sugar and serve.

pasta cake

Torta di vermicelli

SERVES 8

REGION: Emilia-Romagna

avere le mani in pasta.
TO HAVE YOUR HANDS
IN THE PASTA.
(SAID OF A HANDS-ON PERSON.)

Like magic, this fascinating recipe turns half a pound of thin vermicelli or angel hair pasta into a dense, moist cake. At first glance it may look like a noodle pudding recipe, but it's not. Unlike noodles, when thin pasta bakes, it melds into a lush mass of creamy sweetness. The nuts and the crisped top add pleasing crunch.

In a medium saucepan, bring the milk and honey or sugar to a low boil, stirring until dissolved.

Meanwhile, parcook the pasta in plenty of boiling salted water for 2 minutes, so it is very *al dente*. Drain, add to the milk mixture, and simmer until nearly all the milk has been absorbed, about 4 minutes. Taste and add salt, or more honey or sugar, if you like. Let cool to room temperature.

Preheat the oven to 350°F (180°C). Lightly butter a 9-inch (23-centimeter) nonstick pie pan and dust with flour.

In a large bowl, beat the eggs until frothy, then fold in the nuts and the raisins (if using). With a fork, stir in the pasta until well combined. Pour the mixture into the prepared pan and bake for about 35 minutes, until the edges are golden and the center is set.

While still warm, sprinkle the top with the cinnamon and confectioners' sugar. Serve at room temperature or cold.

Milk ✖ 1¼ cups (10 fluid ounces/ 300 milliliters)

Honey or sugar ✖ ⅓ cup (2 fluid ounces/ 60 milliliters)

Vermicelli or angel hair pasta ✖ 8 ounces/ 225 grams

Salt

Butter and flour for the pan

Eggs ✖ 4 large

Chopped walnuts or hazelnuts ✖ ½ cup (2 ounces/55 grams)

Chopped almonds or whole pine nuts ✖ ½ cup (2 ounces/55 grams)

Raisins or dried cherries ✖ ¼ cup (1 ½ ounces/40 grams), optional

Ground cinnamon ✖ ½ teaspoon

Confectioners' sugar

angel hair pasta pie

Torta ricciolina

SERVES 8

REGION: Emilia-Romagna

Angel hair pasta seasoned with chocolate and almonds bakes into one of the most unusual, delicious treats I've ever tasted. To make this classic Bolognese dessert, you absolutely must use fresh, not dried, egg pasta, as it isn't boiled before baking. If making your own pasta seems daunting, buy readymade fresh instead. Just make sure it's egg pasta, the kind with a deep yellow color. Water-and-flour white pasta is simply too dry for this dish.

This is a great make-ahead dessert, as it's much better the day after, once all the flavors have melded.

Grind the almonds and granulated sugar in a food processor until the mixture resembles coarse sand. Pulse in the lemon zest, candied citron, and cocoa powder until well combined. Divide into 3 portions.

Preheat the oven to 350°F (180°C).

Roll the pie crust dough out into a circle large enough to line a 9- to 10-inch (23- to 25-centimeter) pie pan and fit it into the pan. With a fork, pierce the bottom and sides of the crust.

Divide the pasta into 3 portions, with one portion slightly larger than the other two. Line the pie crust with the larger portion of pasta and sprinkle with one portion of the almond mixture. Lift the pasta with the tip of a knife so it is loose and free-form. Do not press the pasta down. Dot the pasta with one third of the butter. Top with another layer of pasta sprinkled with a portion of the almond mixture and more butter. Repeat to make a third layer.

Loosely cover with aluminum foil, bake for 25 minutes, then remove the foil and continue baking uncovered for another 20 to 25 minutes, until the top is golden and the center set.

Remove from the oven and immediately sprinkle the top of the pie with the rum. It will hiss and absorb quickly, with most of the alcohol evaporating, leaving just a lovely aroma and flavor.

Cool to room temperature on a wire rack. Sprinkle with confectioners' sugar and serve, or, preferably, let stand overnight or for 24 hours before serving.

Blanched whole almonds ✖ 1½ cups (8 ounces/225 grams)

Sugar ✖ ¾ cup (5¼ ounces/150 grams)

Grated zest of 1 lemon

A small handful of finely chopped candied citron or candied orange peel

Unsweetened cocoa powder ✖ 1 tablespoon

½ recipe Pie Crust Dough (page 198)

Thin fresh egg pasta, such as tagliatelline or angel hair, store-bought or homemade (page 200) ✖ 8 ounces/225 grams

Butter ✖ 6 tablespoons (3 ounces/85 grams), thinly sliced

Rum ✖ 6 tablespoons

Confectioners' sugar

sicilian sweet meat turnovers

'Mpanatigghi

MAKES ABOUT 2 DOZEN

REGION: Sicily

Meat in a chocolate dessert might seem a little bizarre, but these little empanada-shaped baked Sicilian treats are really tasty. A classic for centuries, they're still sold in pastry shops in Modica and throughout southeastern Sicily. The name, *'mpanatigghia,* comes from the Sicilian corruption of the Spanish *empanada.*

Italy has a long history of combining luxury foods—like pasta and meat—with other luxury foods like sugar and candied fruit. In the 1600s, the New World luxury food chocolate became more available and it, too, was added to such dishes. Legend has it that this dessert was invented at the end of the 1600s by the nuns of the monastery dell' Origlione di Palermo and was offered to pilgrims as a concentrated energy food well suited for their long journey. The chocolate, they thought, helped the meat to stay fresh.

The filling has an amazing texture—dense and velvety—with a deep, rich chocolate flavor. The meat doesn't stand out, but like cocoa butter provides the satisfying lushness that only fats can. Chocolate pairs well with meat in savory dishes (think Mexican mole), so why not in a sweet Italian dessert? The turnovers are wonderful with Barolo Chinato, a spiced red dessert wine especially made for pairing with chocolate.

FOR THE FILLING:

Blanched whole almonds ✖ ¾ cup
(4 ounces/115 grams)

Sugar ✖ 2 cups (14 ounces/400 grams)

Ground veal or beef ✖ 6 ounces/170 grams

Pinch of salt

Dark chocolate, preferably from Modica ✖
½ ounce/15 grams, finely chopped

Unsweetened cocoa powder ✖ ½ cup
(1½ ounces/40 grams)

Ground cinnamon ✖ ½ teaspoon

Pinch of ground cloves

Egg ✖ 1 large

Egg whites ✖ 2 large

Make the filling: Make the filling the day before, or at least several hours in advance, as it tastes best if it's left to rest. In a food processor, combine the almonds and 1 cup (7 ounces/200 grams) of the granulated sugar and grind until the mixture resembles fine sand. Set aside.

In a skillet, cook the ground meat with the salt over very, very low heat, breaking up the meat into small pieces, until light pink. Do not overcook. Remove from the heat and transfer to a large bowl. Stir in the almond-sugar mixture, the remaining 1 cup granulated sugar, the chocolate, cocoa powder, cinnamon, cloves, and whole egg until well combined.

In a medium bowl, using a whisk or electric mixer, beat the eggs whites until stiff peaks form. Stir the whites into the meat mixture until you have a well-combined paste. Cover with plastic wrap and refrigerate until ready to use.

Make the dough: Combine the flour, sugar, and lard in a large bowl and mix with your fingers until the mixture resembles fine sand. Mix in the egg yolks and baking powder and knead, adding a little water if needed, to form a dough. Cover with plastic wrap and refrigerate for at least 30 minutes.

Assemble the turnovers: Preheat the oven to 400°F (200°C). Line a baking sheet with parchment paper.

Roll the dough out to ⅛ inch (3 millimeters) thick on a floured work surface. Add more flour if the dough is too sticky. Using a 4-inch (10-centimeter) round cookie cutter, cut out dough circles.

Place about 1 tablespoon of the chocolate-meat mixture in the center of each circle. Brush half of the dough edge with water, then fold the dough over and pinch the edges to seal. Put on the prepared baking sheet. Repeat with the remaining dough and filling.

Brush the top of the turnovers with the egg white. Cut a little vent in the top of the pastry—either a V shape with scissors or an X with a sharp knife—so the filling can expand without breaking through the sealed edges of the dough. Bake for about 20 minutes, until light golden.

Sprinkle with confectioners' sugar and serve warm or at room temperature.

FOR THE DOUGH:

All-purpose flour ✖ 2½ cups
(11¼ ounces/315 grams)

Sugar ✖ ¾ cup (5¼ ounces/150 grams)

Lard or butter ✖ 5 tablespoons
(2½ ounces/70 grams)

Egg yolks ✖ 2 large

Baking powder ✖ 1 teaspoon

Egg white ✖ 1 large

Confectioners' sugar

CHAPTER EIGHT

holiday

LE FESTE

pandoro christmas tree cake

SERVES 10

REGION: Veneto and popular throughout Italy

Pandoro, a tall star-shaped cake, has a delicious eggy briochelike soft center, with a lovely vanilla-butter aroma. In Italy, *pandoro* is often served cut in horizontal slices that are restacked to look like a Christmas tree. It even comes boxed with a packet of confectioners' sugar to sprinkle on top.

    Pandoro, in its present-day form, first appeared in late-nineteenth-century Verona. There are two different legends about its origin. The first dates *pandoro*'s birth to the Renaissance and to the custom of Venetian bakers dusting gold leaf onto cone-shaped cakes called *pan de oro,* "bread of gold," for their wealthy customers. The second legend assigns a humbler origin to *pandoro,* suggesting that it might have descended from a star-shaped homemade cake, *nadalin,* enjoyed by Verona's farmers during Christmas. Here, the cake is taken to another level: Each layer is spread with mascarpone custard and decorated with candies.

In a small saucepan, combine ¼ cup (2 fluid ounces/60 milliliters) water and ¼ cup (1¾ ounces/50 grams) of the granulated sugar and bring to a boil. Remove from the heat and stir in 4 tablespoons of the liqueur. Set aside.

In a medium bowl, with an electric mixer, beat the egg yolks and the remaining ½ cup (3½ ounces/100 grams) granulated sugar for about 5 minutes, until light yellow and fluffy. Beat in the remaining 2 tablespoons liqueur, then fold in the mascarpone.

In a separate medium bowl, whip the cream until firm peaks form. Fold the mascarpone mixture into the whipped cream.

Carefully, so as not to break the points, cut the *pandoro* horizontally into 6 slices. Brush the outsides of the slices (the browned parts) with the liqueur syrup.

Place the largest *pandoro* slice on a serving platter and spread with some of the mascarpone mixture. Cover with the next largest slice, angling it so that the points of the star don't line up. Spread with some of the mascarpone mixture and repeat with the remaining layers, finishing with a dollop of mascarpone on top.

Decorate the points with candies or candied cherries and mint leaves. Sprinkle the entire cake with confectioners' sugar and serve.

NOTE: *Pandoro* is available in many supermarkets beginning in the late fall. Thanks to the natural yeast used in making *pandoro,* and despite containing no artificial preservatives, it lasts more than six months without refrigeration.

Sugar ✳ ¾ cup (5¼ ounces/150 grams)

Liqueur, such as Cointreau, or rum ✳ 6 tablespoons

Egg yolks ✳ 2 large

Mascarpone cheese ✳ 14 ounces/400 grams

Heavy cream ✳ 1 cup (8 fluid ounces/ 240 milliliters)

Pandoro (see Note) ✳ 1 cake (about 1 pound/ 455 grams)

Candied cherries, fresh mint leaves, silver confetti, and crushed candy canes for decoration

Confectioners' sugar

For me—probably you, too, since you're reading this—Italy's food traditions are precious. Certain products and recipes are so definitively Italian that their origins, recipes, and even names are worth protecting and preserving. When it comes to Italy's sweets and pasta, that's AIDEPI's job.

AIDEPI—Associazione delle Industrie del Dolce e della Pasta Italiane (the Association of Italian Dessert and Pasta Manufacturers)—is an organization that promotes the Italian sweets and pasta industries, educates the world about it, and, most intriguingly, sets forth regulations that cover the processes and ingredients permitted for various products. Their standards, it turns out, are some of the world's strictest.

Italy's sweet tradition dates back to ancient Roman times. Then, as today, the emphasis was on pure desserts that reflect a simple cuisine using local ingredients, especially Italy's rich grains, regional honey, flavorful eggs and butter, and the country's best nuts and fruits. AIDEPI, founded in 1967, works hard to ensure that those ancient traditions persist. According to AIDEPI director Mario Piccialuti, "Prior to AIDEPI's efforts, substandard 'Made in Italy' cake products labeled 'Pandoro' were available that contained inferior or insufficient amounts of the ingredients that distinguish the buttery sweet taste of true pandoro. The difference in flavor is easy to detect, and the increasing spread of such 'counterfeit' cakes threatened to destroy the public's faith in the pandoro name and quality. AIDEPI helped put in place regulations to preserve their purity, recipe, and flavor, and set strict criteria for both ingredients and manufacturing process." Other similarly designated and regulated sweets include amaretti and savoiardi cookies, and colomba and panettone cakes.

For example, to qualify as authentic, panettone, the famous holiday cake, must follow a definitive checklist in accordance with its DOP (Denominazione di Origine Protetta) status. Ingredients must be region-specific, and only the best butter—and a guaranteed amount of it—may be used. There are required quantities of eggs and raisins and the dough may contain only natural yeast. All this and a manufacturing process that takes literally forty hours for a single cake. Almost painfully rigorous, but the result is squisito—exquisite!

AIDEPI's defense of the integrity of the "Made in Italy" marking and product quality appeals to me, so when they invited me to serve as their first "ambassador" in the United States and to create their first American-targeted website (dolceitalia.com), I was pleased to accept.

christmas walnut macaroni

Maccheroni natalizi con le noci

SERVES 4 TO 6

REGION: Umbria

natale viene una volta all'anno.

CHRISTMAS COMES JUST ONCE A YEAR.

A mound of luscious pasta tossed in a sweet dark chocolate sauce and topped with grated chocolate, this traditional Christmas Eve dessert is far too delectable to enjoy just once a year! It's shockingly simple to make: Just toss cooked pasta with a few ingredients that you probably already have in your pantry and top with shaved chocolate. An unusual, easy, satisfying, and homey dessert that is not too sweet or heavy.

Fresh pasta, such as pappadelle or fettuccine ✕ 10 ounces/280 grams

Sugar ✕ 1/2 cup (3 1/2 ounces/100 grams)

Dark chocolate ✕ 2 ounces/55 grams, finely chopped

Finely chopped walnuts ✕ 1 cup (4 ounces/115 grams)

Rum ✕ 3 tablespoons

Grated zest of 1/2 lemon

Ground cinnamon

Freshly grated nutmeg

Honey

Cook the pasta in water according to the package directions. Drain, return to the cooking pot, and, off the heat, immediately toss with the sugar, chocolate, walnuts, rum, lemon zest, and a pinch each of cinnamon and nutmeg. Toss well, until the sugar is dissolved and the chocolate is melted.

Transfer to a serving platter and let cool to room temperature, but do not refrigerate. Top with grated chocolate and a drizzle of honey and serve.

neapolitan honey treats

Struffoli in cestino di croccante

SERVES 10 TO 12

REGION: Campania

Struffoli, traditional Carnival and Christmas treats, are marble-sized fried dough balls dipped in honey, piled into a mound, and topped with colored sugar and candied fruit. It's a festive communally shared dessert that's put out to encourage guests to stay at the table to chat and nibble.

Struffoli can be fried or baked and make a cheerful centerpiece just as they are, heaped onto a serving plate. Or, as they do in Naples, serve them in an edible candy dish. Both the candy dish and the *stuffoli* are actually fun and very easy to make.

All-purpose flour ✳ 2½ cups (11¼ ounces/315 grams)

Sugar ✳ 5 tablespoons (2¼ ounces/ 65 grams)

Baking soda ✳ 1½ teaspoons

Salt ✳ ¼ teaspoon

Eggs ✳ 4 large

Egg yolks ✳ 2 large

Butter ✳ 4 tablespoons (2 ounces/55 grams), melted

Cointreau or limoncello ✳ 3 tablespoons

Pure vanilla extract ✳ 1 tablespoon

Grated zest of 2 lemons

Grated zest of 1 orange

Sunflower or other vegetable oil for frying

Honey ✳ 1 cup (8 ounces/240 milliliters)

Diavolilli (tiny colored sugar balls), candied cherries, confetti, assorted sugar-coated nuts, and so on, optional

Edible Candy Dish, optional; recipe follows

In a large bowl, with an electric mixer, combine the flour, 3 tablespoons of the sugar, the baking soda, salt, 4 whole eggs, 2 egg yolks, the butter, liqueur, vanilla, and the lemon and orange zests until a dough forms. Refrigerate for 30 minutes.

Take a small handful of the dough and roll it into a rope about ¾-inch (18 millimeters) thick. Cut the dough into hazelnut-sized sections about ½ inch (12 millimeters) thick. Fill a heavy, deep saucepan with 3 inches (7.5 centimeters) of oil and heat over medium-high heat. Working in batches, add the dough pieces and fry until golden. Drain on a paper towel–lined plate. Repeat with the remaining dough. (Alternatively, you can bake them. See Note.)

In a small saucepan, combine the honey and the remaining 2 table-spoons sugar and heat until runny. Remove from the heat and stir in the fried balls, a few at a time, and turn until they are well coated in the honey mixture. Using a slotted spoon, remove the coated balls and arrange them in a circle in a shallow bowl. Repeat with the remaining dough balls, adding them to the pile to form a tall mound. Pour any remaining honey over the top and decorate with a scattering of colored sugar balls, confetti, and candied fruit, if you like. The dessert is best if served within 24 hours and traditionally is placed in the center of the table so that guests may help themselves with their fingers.

NOTE: To bake the dough pieces, place them about 1 inch (2.5 centi-meters) apart on a well-greased baking sheet and bake at 400°F (200°C) for about 7 minutes. Turn the balls and bake on the other side for another 6 to 7 minutes, until light golden. They will not be as round or as nicely golden as the fried version, but the taste will be just as stupendous. You may like to try baking half the dough and frying half, to give your *struffoli* color gradations.

edible candy dish

Don't panic, this isn't hard to do. The candy dish is really just a big blob of almond brittle flattened into the shape of a plate.

Lightly oil a large nonstick baking sheet. Lightly oil the inside of a large pie pan, shallow bowl, or mold.

In a heavy saucepan, heat the corn syrup over medium-high heat until warm, then stir in the sugar. At first the sugar just sort of sits there, but it will start to become translucent in 3 to 4 minutes, then turn ivory-colored for another 3 minutes or so, and then finally darken and become liquidy.

Continue cooking, stirring occasionally with an oil-coated wooden spoon, until the syrup is a rich golden color, about 12 minutes. Remove from the heat and stir in the almonds.

Carefully, as the sugar is scorching hot, pour the mixture onto the prepared baking sheet. Using a rolling pin, gently flatten the mixture and roll it out into a large thin circle at least 13 inches (33 centimeters) in diameter. Once it has cooled a little and seems firm, fit the circle into the prepared mold. Let harden and cool to room temperature, then remove from the mold.

Vegetable or olive oil for the baking sheet and pan

Corn syrup ✕ 4 tablespoons

Sugar ✕ 2¼ cups (15¾ ounces/450 grams)

Sliced almonds ✕ 2 cups (8 ounces/ 225 grams)

confetti

Confetti, sugar-coated almonds, are used to top desserts, offered as party favors, and added to flower and fruit baskets. Over the years Italians have even developed a color code—white sugar-coated almonds for weddings, green for engagements, silver for twenty-fifth anniversaries, blue or pink for christenings, and red for graduations.

There are also sugar-coated spices and herbs, from rosemary leaves and lavender buds to anise seeds, eaten as after-dinner palate cleansers or added to cakes or cookies as decorative toppings. Sugar-coated fennel seeds are often given as a gift to new mothers to help with nursing.

Romanengo, a Genoa confectionery shop, has been making confetti and candied fruit since 1780, and still today manufactures everything by hand in small batches. "Confection is an art form, and has a long history here in Genoa, a port that was one of the first to receive sugar into Europe," explains Pietro Romanengo, one of the current generation's five Romanengo brothers. To create their amazingly delicate cinnamon confetti, Giovanni Battista Romanengo, another brother, personally hand snips the finest Ceylon cinnamon bark into thin wisps with shears. He places about 20 pounds (9 kilograms) of the cinnamon snippets into the slowly rotating panning machine (which looks like a copper cement mixer) that coats them in sugar syrup, drop by drop through a suspended funnel, over the course of two days.

Stratta, a sweets shop in Turin, sells traditional Italian confetti in a range of innovative newer flavors, including cardamom, cumin, coriander, rosemary, and rye. There's a Confetti Museum open to the public in the Pelino factory in Sulmona, a town in Abruzzo in the province of L'Aquila. And one of Italy's largest makers of confetti is Crispo, located in Naples.

honey-drenched "roses"

Carteddate

MAKES ABOUT 2 DOZEN

REGION: Puglia

solo quando friggi senti l'odore.

ONLY WHILE IT'S FRYING CAN YOU SMELL IT. (TO TRULY UNDERSTAND SOMETHING, YOU NEED FIRSTHAND EXPERIENCE.)

This crunchy honey-drenched sweet is one of the most popular desserts of southern Italy, and is always served at Christmas and during Carnival season. You'll get a kick out of making these—it's kind of like a combination arts and crafts project and cooking adventure. Long strips of pasta dough are twirled and pinched to form pretty rose shapes. It only takes making one or two to get the hang of it.

All-purpose flour ✕ 3¼ cups (16 ounces/ 455 grams)

White wine ✕ ½ cup (4 fluid ounces/ 120 milliliters)

Olive oil ✕ ⅓ cup (2½ fluid ounces/ 75 milliliters), plus more for frying

Egg ✕ 1 large

Honey ✕ 1 cup (8 fluid ounces/ 240 milliliters)

Ground cinnamon

Ground cloves

Mosto cotto vino cotto, or *vin santo*, optional

Sift the flour into a large bowl or onto a work surface and make a well in the center. Fill the well with the wine, oil, and egg. Incorporate the flour, a little at a time, working from the center out, until a dough forms. If the dough is dry, add a few drops of warm water. Knead the dough until smooth and silky to the touch. Put in a resealable plastic bag or wrap in plastic wrap and let rest for 15 minutes.

Divide the dough into 4 portions. Start with one section, keeping the rest in the bag or wrapped in plastic wrap. Using a pasta machine or rolling pin, roll the dough out into a rectangle ⅛ inch (3 millimeters) thick, about 15 inches (38 centimeters) long, and 6 to 7 inches (15 to 17 centimeters) wide. Using a knife, or preferably a curly-edged ravioli cutter, cut strips about 1¼ inches (3 centimeters) wide and about 15 inches (38 centimeters) long.

To make a *carteddate*, take one of the strips and, beginning at one end, bring the edges of the dough together and pinch. Pinch again, 2 inches (5 centimeters) down, to create a little almond-shaped pocket. Make a few more pockets, and then begin coiling the dough around itself, connecting the coils by pinching the pockets together at the widest point. Keep pinching and coiling until you get to the end of the strip of dough, then pinch that against the coil to seal. This should produce a circle about 3½ inches (9 centimeters) in diameter. Repeat with all the remaining dough. Let the *carteddate* rest, covered with a cotton dishcloth, overnight.

The *carteddate* can then be fried or baked. If you are frying them, heat about 1 inch (2.5 centimeters) of oil in a small, deep frying pan until very hot but not smoking. Fry the *carteddate* one or two at a time, turning them, until golden, about 20 seconds on the first side and 10 seconds on the second side. Do not overcook. They should just be lightly golden. Drain on a paper towel–lined plate, rose side down.

If you are baking them, put the *carteddate* on a lightly oiled baking sheet and bake at 400°F (200°C) for about 20 minutes, then turn them over and continue baking for about 5 minutes longer, or until golden.

Warm the honey in a small saucepan and dip each *carteddate* in the honey. Put them on a serving plate and sprinkle with cinnamon and cloves to taste and the *mosto cotto*, if you like. They are also terrific without honey, just sprinkled with sugar.

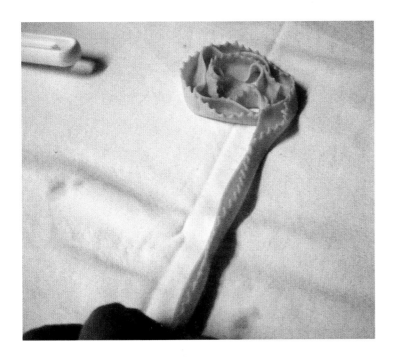

carnival crisps

Cenci

MAKES ABOUT 5 DOZEN

REGION: Throughout Italy

Bet you can't eat just one! Crunchy wisps, feather-light, generously sprinkled with confectioners' sugar—this is the classic Carnival treat. They're found in various regions of Italy, under one cute name or another—*chiacchiere* (chatter), *zacarette* (shavings), *cenci* (rags), or *bugie* (lies)—each seasoned with the area's local specialty wine or liqueur. The secret to making these treats light and absolutely, totally nongreasy is to roll the dough paper-thin.

Put the flour in a large bowl and make a well in the center. To the well, add the eggs, butter, sugar, salt, and Marsala. Gradually incorporate the flour into the center liquids, working with your fingers, until a dough forms. If the dough is too dry, add a few more drops of Marsala; if too moist, sprinkle with a bit more flour. Knead the dough for at least 5 minutes, until smooth and elastic. Cover the bowl with a clean dishcloth and let rest at room temperature for 1 hour. (This is key to getting those pretty little bubbles on the dough when you fry it.)

Working in small batches, run the dough through a pasta machine, starting at the thickest opening and ending at the thinnest. Lay the strips of thin dough on a clean cotton canvas cloth or lightly floured work surface.

Cut the dough into whatever shapes you like, using either a curly-edged ravioli cutter or a knife. They can be rectangular, triangular, irregular, anything! One of the common shapes is a rectangle about 3½ inches long by 2 inches wide (9 by 5 centimeters) with a 2-inch (5-centimeter) slit in the center.

Pour 1 inch (2.5 centimeters) of oil into a deep pot and heat it to 335°F (170°C) or until hot enough that a small bit of thin dough dropped into the oil will rise within a second or two. Fry the dough in batches until just barely golden. (They fry very quickly because they are so thin.) Drain on a paper towel–lined plate. Dust both sides with lots of confectioners' sugar and serve at room temperature.

All-purpose flour ✕ 1½ cups (6 ounces/ 170 grams), plus more as needed

Eggs ✕ 2 large

Butter ✕ 2 tablespoons, diced

Sugar ✕ 2 tablespoons

Salt ✕ ½ teaspoon

Marsala wine ✕ 2 tablespoons

Grated zest of 1 lemon or ½ orange

Sunflower or light vegetable oil

Confectioners' sugar

"instant" rum babà panettone

SERVES 8 TO 12

REGION: Lombardy and throughout Italy

Tall and dome-shaped, *panettone* is a soft, sweet yeast cake with the fruity aroma of raisins and candied oranges.

It's the quintessential Italian Christmas dessert, never absent from the Italian holiday table. *Panettone* is usually served plain, accompanied by a glass of Asti Spumante, but also makes a great base for many delicious treats, including bread pudding and French toast. One of my favorite ways to serve *panettone* is drenched in rum syrup, making a virtually instant babà cake.

Panettone imported from Italy is available beginning in the fall at many supermarkets. Available in standard 1- and 2-pound (455- and 910-gram) sizes, *panettone* also comes in adorable single-serving-sized portions, which work especially well with this recipe.

Sugar ✖ 3 cups (21 ounces/600 grams)

Dark rum ✖ ¼ to ½ cup (2 to 4 fluid ounces/60 to 120 milliliters)

Panettone ✖ 8 slices or 8 small individual-sized *panettone*

Confectioners' sugar

Fresh or frozen berries, optional

In a medium saucepan, combine the sugar and 1½ cups (12 fluid ounces/360 milliliters) water and bring to a boil. Lower the heat and simmer until thickened, about 15 minutes. Remove from the heat. Stir in the rum to taste. Let cool to room temperature.

Arrange the *panettone* on a serving platter. An hour before serving, slowly pour the rum syrup over the *panettone* so that all the liquid is absorbed.

Serve topped with confectioners' sugar and accompanied by berries, if you like.

in italy

Although *panettone* probably originated in Milan in the fifteenth century, it's current distinctive dome shape dates only to the 1920s. *Panettone* has spawned many legends. The most popular concerns a young Milanese nobleman, a member of the Atellini family, who fell in love with the daughter of a baker named Toni. To impress the girl's father, the young man disguised himself as a baker's assistant and invented a new, fruitcakelike bread. People came to the bakery in droves to purchase the magnificent new creation dubbed *Pan de Toni* ("Tony's bread"). A variation of the legend has Toni saving the day by inventing the bread as a quick replacement for a dessert that had burned while being prepared for a Christmas feast held by the duke of Milan, Ludovico Sforza.

bauli, italy's foremost panettone maker

Founded in 1937 by Ruggero Bauli as a small artisanal bakeshop, the Bauli company today occupies roughly five million square feet, makes more than one thousand products, and is Italy's leading maker of holiday cakes—*panettone*, *pandoro*, and *colomba*.

Visiting Bauli's headquarters in the month of November, I was able to observe the fascinating production process. Vast vats of dough and endless long rows of uncooked *panettone* progressing through cavernous ovens like an army of squat soldiers marching along a fiery orange landscape. Labyrinthian mechanical pathways of cakes snaking along what seem like miles of computer-controlled conveyors, which lead to a final packing operation performed by powerful robots with quick, long arms that gently place the final product into shipping cartons.

The Bauli tour is a study in contrasts—from the football field–sized high-tech production lines to the one-room closet-sized heart of the operation where the "mother" dough is cultivated and protected, a persistent reminder of the company's artisanal origins. That little room reminded me of a hospital nursery. A few dedicated workers dressed in white lab coats daily rotate and "massage" each cradle of yeast. It must be attended twenty-four hours a day,

seven days a week. They're looking after the "mother"—a precious nucleus of fermented dough that is refreshed daily with water and flour. Bits of the mother are removed and placed into bassinet-like containers, where they are carefully nurtured for forty days. Each lump of yeast is snugly swaddled in cloth, and will grow up to become the leavening for about five hundred loaves of *panettone* or *pandoro*. The lovingly cultivated yeast is the secret of the cake's amazingly long shelf life and wonderfully smooth texture. It isn't just me that sees these bundles of yeast as the company's babies. In 1996, there was a fire at the Bauli plant. The staff sprang into action and saved the little bits of the "mother," bringing them to their own homes. They knew it was more critical to the company than any production line or machine. As one of the workers told me, "The 'mother' yeast was born here, and it's part of the Bauli family."

Panettone making follows an extraordinarily elaborate and time-consuming process—taking more than forty hours. It's kneaded and left to rise several times before baking, with flour, eggs, butter, sugar, and candied fruit added in stages. At last, after each cake has been allowed to rise in its own little paper container, it's baked, cooled, wrapped in plastic, packed up by hand, and sent on its way.

panettone sweet tweets

- CARAMELIZED PANETTONE: Melt butter in a skillet. Sprinkle *panettone* with grappa and sugar on both sides, fry, flip, and serve warm.
- PANETTONE BREAD PUDDING: Layer *panettone*, beaten eggs, cream, sugar, dollops of jam, mascarpone, chopped chocolate, and/or fruit. Bake at 350°F (180°C) until cooked through.
- PANETTONE "BELLINI": In a serving glass, layer slices of *panettone*, splash with prosecco or Asti Spumante, and top with peaches and whipped cream.
- ICE CREAM CAKE: Hollow out a *panettone*, fill with ice cream, and freeze. Serve with toppings. (Use the center for the desserts above.)
- PANETTONE PANINI: Toast and slather with Nutella. Or fill slices with chopped dark chocolate and toast in a *panini* press.

donut with a cherry on top

Zeppole di San Giuseppe al forno

MAKES 6 LARGE OR 12 MINI DONUTS

REGION: Campania, especially Naples

This eggy-rich donut, served with thick vanilla custard and topped with a cherry, is a traditional treat prepared every March 19 for the Feast of San Giuseppe, St. Joseph's Day. Although often fried, here they are baked, making them light enough for you to add a double plop of custard and an extra cherry on top!

FOR THE CUSTARD AND CHERRIES:

Pitted cherries, fresh or frozen (see Note) ✳ 12 large

Sugar ✳ ½ cup (3½ ounces/100 grams), plus more for the cherries

Milk ✳ 1⅔ cups (13½ fluid ounces/ 405 milliliters)

Heavy cream ✳ ⅓ cup (2½ fluid ounces/ 75 milliliters)

Egg yolks ✳ 6 large

Potato starch ✳ ¼ cup (1 ounces/30 grams)

Grated zest of ½ lemon

½ vanilla bean, grated on a Microplane

Salt ✳ ¼ teaspoon

FOR THE DONUTS:

Butter ✳ 6 tablespoons (3 ounces/85 grams)

Salt ✳ ¼ teaspoon

All-purpose flour ✳ 1 cup (4½ ounces/ 130 grams)

Eggs ✳ 4 large

Make the custard and candied cherries: Combine the cherries and their weight in sugar in a small saucepan and refrigerate for 8 hours or overnight. Heat over very low heat for about 10 minutes, until they soften slightly, then transfer to a small bowl and let cool to room temperature. Refrigerate until ready to use.

In a saucepan over medium heat, bring the milk and cream to a low boil.

Meanwhile, in a bowl, with an electric mixer, beat the egg yolks, ½ cup (3½ ounces/100 grams) sugar, the potato starch, lemon zest, vanilla, and salt until smooth and creamy. Pour in the hot milk and beat until combined. Return the mixture back to the saucepan and heat over medium-low heat, beating constantly, until the mixture thickens, about 3 minutes.

Immediately pour the mixture into a bowl and let cool to room temperature. Cover with plastic wrap, with the wrap touching the custard to prevent a skin from forming, and refrigerate until ready to use.

Make the donuts: Preheat the oven to 375°F (190°C). Line a large baking sheet with parchment paper.

In a medium saucepan, combine 1 cup (8 fluid ounces/237 milliliters) water, the butter, and salt and bring to a boil, stirring until the butter melts. Remove from the heat and add the flour, beating vigorously with a wooden spoon until combined. The dough will be very dense.

Return the pan to low heat and stir rapidly until the flour absorbs all the liquid and forms a ball, pulling away from the sides of the pan. Continue stirring until a film forms on the bottom of the pan and the dough is no longer sticky, about 2 minutes. Remove from the heat and add the eggs to the dough, one at a time, beating vigorously with a wooden spoon or electric mixer after each addition. The dough will look like lumpy cottage cheese, but that's normal. Continue adding the eggs, beating with each addition, until the dough is thick and smooth.

Put the dough in a pastry bag with a large star nozzle, or into a sturdy plastic bag with a corner cut off, and pipe out 6 large (3-inch-/ 7.5-centimeter-diameter) or 12 small (1½-inch/4-centimeter) donut shapes. Regardless of which size, pipe a double layer of dough for each donut, one layer of dough over the other. Bake for about 25 minutes, until golden.

Cool to room temperature on wire racks. To serve, generously fill the center hole with custard and put a cherry on top.

NOTE: Instead of making your own candied cherries, substitute amarena cherries in syrup, found in jars and available online or at specialty grocers.

the feast of san giuseppe

The Feast of San Giuseppe, March 19, is a religious holiday in Italy and also the day Italians celebrate Father's Day, *Festa del Papá*. In some parts of Italy, school-age children secretly hide a letter—filled with appreciation and promises of good behavior—under Dad's dinner plate. There is no traditional Father's Day dessert, just the dad's favorites. However, there are many special regional desserts for the Feast of San Giuseppe, including:

- *Bigné di San Giuseppe*: A specialty of Rome, fried dough filled with cream or chocolate.

- *Frittelle di riso*: Fried balls of sweetened rice pudding.

- *Sfinge di San Giuseppe*: Fried dough puffs topped with sweetened ricotta.

colomba easter zuppa inglese

SERVES 8

REGION: Veneto, and throughout Italy

*dire che pasqua
viene di venerdi.*

TO SAY THAT EASTER FALLS ON A
THURSDAY. (TO DENY THE OBVIOUS.)

You can make *zuppa inglese* with all sorts of readymade cookies or cakes. Here it's made with *colomba,* Italy's traditional Easter cake. I love *colomba*'s soft yeasty cake texture and fabulous buttery aroma. My favorite part is the top of the cake, which has a crisp, sweet almond crust.

In Italy, the day after Easter is called *Pasquetta,* "Little Easter," or *Il Lunedi dell'Angelo,* "Angel's Monday." Italians traditionally go on a picnic that day, the first outdoor excursion since the start of winter. Dessert includes all the leftover Easter sweets like *pastiera, colomba* cake, or Easter eggs.

Colomba, preferably Bauli brand (see Sources, page 203) �֍ 16 ounces/455 grams

Frozen peaches ✖ 1 pound/455 grams, thawed

Apricot or peach jam ✖ 1 cup (8 fluid ounces/240 milliliters)

Sweet liqueur, such as limoncello, or apricot or peach juice ✖ ½ cup (4 fluid ounces/ 120 milliliters)

Ricotta cheese ✖ 2 cups (about 18 ounces/500 grams)

Mascarpone cheese ✖ 8 ounces/225 grams

Sugar ✖ 6 tablespoons

Whipped cream

Chocolate Italian Easter eggs, broken into pieces

Cut the cake into ½-inch (12-millimeter) slices.

In a bowl, combine the peaches with the jam and liqueur and stir until the jam is liquidy.

In another bowl, beat the ricotta, mascarpone, and sugar until smooth and creamy. Fold in whipped cream to taste.

Line the bottom of a 2-quart (2-liter) glass bowl with cake pieces. Top with some of the peaches and their liquid. Spread with a layer of the whipped cream mixture and sprinkle with chocolate. Repeat the layers, ending with the whipped cream mixture on top and reserving some of the cake for garnish. Cover with plastic wrap and refrigerate for at least 4 hours or overnight.

Garnish with more chocolate and diced pieces of cake just before serving.

lover's lemon-spice cake

Ciaramicola

SERVES 8 TO 10.

REGION: Umbria, especially Perugia

I like this recipe for several reasons: First, it's got a cute backstory. *Ciaramicola* is traditionally exchanged between families and loved ones, and it's customary for a woman to give one to her fiancé on Easter morning as a symbol of her love. Second, it's really pretty. Red-tinged cake with lovely fluffy white meringue icing sprinkled with colored sugar. And most important, it's scrumptious, spicy sweet with a hint of lemon.

With its red and white colors matching the city's flag, *ciaramicola* is an unofficial symbol of Perugia.

Butter ✕ ¾ cup (1½ sticks/ 6 ounces/170 grams)

All-purpose flour ✕ 3 cups (13½ ounces/ 385 grams)

Eggs ✕ 2 large

Egg yolks ✕ 3 large

Sugar ✕ 1 cup (7 ounces/200 grams)

Baking powder ✕ 2 teaspoons

Baking soda ✕ 1 teaspoon

Grated zest and juice of 1 lemon

Alchermes (page 182) ✕ ½ cup (4 fluid ounces/120 milliliters)

Salt ✕ ½ teaspoon

Egg whites ✕ 3 large

Confectioners' sugar ✕ 1¼ cups (4¼ ounces/120 grams)

Nonpareils (tiny multicolored sugar balls)

Preheat the oven to 350°F (180°C). Butter and flour a tube cake pan.

In a large bowl, with an electric mixer, beat the eggs, egg yolks, and granulated sugar until smooth and creamy. Add the butter and beat until creamy. Add the baking powder, baking soda, lemon zest and juice, liqueur, and salt and beat until combined. Sift in the flour, a little at a time, combining with a wooden spoon, until a thick batter forms.

Spoon the batter into the prepared pan and let rest for 30 minutes so it can rise and settle into the pan. Bake for 35 to 40 minutes, until a toothpick inserted in the center comes out clean. Slide a knife around the edges of the cake and carefully turn it out onto a baking sheet. Turn the heat off in the oven, but keep the oven door closed.

Meanwhile, just a few minutes before the cake is ready to come out of the oven, make the meringue topping: In a large bowl, with an electric mixer, beat the egg whites and confectioners' sugar until a glossy, dense meringue forms. Top the baked cake with the meringue, sprinkle with the sugar balls, and return to the warm oven until the topping dries and sets, about 15 minutes.

Remove from the oven and serve warm.

easter treats

In Italy, chocolate eggs, *uova di Pasqua,* are very popular. The eggs range from tiny solid ones to foot-high beautifully wrapped hollow eggs with a gift inside. There are eggs for children filled with toys, and those for adults might contain jewelry, designer sunglasses, or various collectibles. Most chocolate shops in Italy will insert custom items into Easter eggs. The customer brings the gift to the shop—anything from an engagement ring to a cell phone or a black lace nightie—and waits while it's encased in a chocolate egg.

Italy's Easter cake is *colomba,* "dove," a bird-shaped sweet yeast cake traditionally filled with candied orange peel and topped with almonds and grains of sugar. Numerous myths surround *colomba* cake. According to one particularly dramatic story, on Easter Day in 1176, the city of Milan was defending itself against invaders. At one point, with the Milanese on the verge of losing, three doves flew over the city. At that moment, the battle shifted and the invaders were vanquished. Legend holds that after that victory the Milanese celebrated by eating cakes shaped like the savior doves.

neapolitan easter pie

Pastiera

SERVES 8 TO 10

REGION: Campania

This traditional ricotta and whole-grain pie has a mouthwatering aroma so distinctive that if you were to wave a slice near any blindfolded Neapolitan, he could instantly identify it. *Pastiera* is prepared in special pans whose edges angle out slightly. The pie is always given away as a gift and, equally important, also always served in the pan it was baked in.

Italian traditionalists say it takes ten days to make, from start to finish: eight days for the grain to soak and cook, and two days for the *pastiera* to rest so all the flavors can properly meld. In fact, traditionally the final preparation is done on Good Friday so it can rest and be ready for Easter Sunday. *Pastiera* used to be exclusively an Easter dessert, but became so popular it's now available year round in Naples. My favorite comes from Mazzaro Pasticceria in Naples.

FOR THE FILLING, PART 1:

Jarred *grano cotto per pastiera* or cooked wheat berries ✳ 1 cup (7 ounces/200 grams)

Milk ✳ 2 cups (16 fluid ounces/480 milliliters)

Grated zest of ½ orange

Grated zest of 1 lemon

Lard or butter ✳ 1 tablespoon

Sugar ✳ 1 tablespoon

Ricotta ✳ 9 ounces/255 grams

Superfine sugar ✳ ⅔ cup (4½ ounces/130 grams)

FOR THE CRUST:

1 recipe Pie Crust Dough (page 198), shaped into a single ball

Butter and potato starch or cornstarch

Make the filling, part 1: Put the *grano cotto*, milk, orange and lemon zests, lard, and granulated sugar in a bowl and set it over a larger pot partially filled with simmering water. Simmer, covered, over low heat, stirring often, until the mixture is dense and creamy about 1 hour. Refrigerate, covered with plastic wrap, for 24 hours.

Press the ricotta through a fine-mesh sieve into a bowl. Add the superfine sugar and beat with a fork or whisk for 5 or 6 minutes, until creamy. Cover and refrigerate for 24 hours.

Make the crust: Refrigerate the wrapped dough for at least 1 hour, or until ready to use.

Preheat the oven to 350°F (180°C). Lightly butter a 9½-inch (23-centimeter) round cake pan and dust with potato starch.

On a work surface dusted with potato starch, roll two thirds of the dough out into a circle large enough to line the pan. Fit it into the prepared pan and gently press into the bottom and up the sides of the pan. Trim the excess dough flush with the top edge of the pan. With a fork, pierce the bottom and sides of the crust all over. Set aside.

Make the filling, part 2: Add the ricotta to the *grano cotto* and mix with a wooden spoon until combined. Add the egg yolks, candied peel, and *aroma di millefiore* and mix until combined.

In a separate bowl, whisk the egg whites with a whisk or electric mixer until soft peaks form. Gently fold the whites into the ricottta mixture until combined. Pour the mixture into the crust.

Roll the remaining dough out into a large circle. Using a knife or pastry cutter or curly-edged ravioli cutter, cut long ½-inch-wide (12-millimeter-wide) strips of dough. Lay the strips in a lattice pattern over the top of the filling. Trim the excess dough across the top edge of the pan. Bake for 30 minutes, then turn the *pastiera* so it bakes evenly, lower the oven temperature to 340°F (170°C), and bake for 30 to 40 minutes longer, until the filling is glossy and the crust is light golden. The center will still be jiggly, but it will set as it cools.

Cool to room temperature in the pan. Refrigerate for at least 24 hours before serving. Serve at room temperature, right from the pan, topped with a light sprinkling of confectioners' sugar.

FOR THE FILLING, PART 2:

Eggs ✳ 3 large, separated

Candied orange peel, finely chopped ✳ ½ cup (3½ ounces/100 grams)

Aroma di millefiori ✳ ½ teaspoon or a few drops of orange blossom water

Confectioners' sugar

after-dinner beverages

BEVANDE DOPO CENA

Italians like to linger at the dinner table, eating slowly and chatting. Dessert too is leisurely and often served in three parts, as a way to keep guests at the table, to keep conversation going. First the sweet itself is served, accompanied by a dessert wine or liqueur. Next comes espresso, butunlike in the States, in Italy coffee or tea is served only after the dessert is eaten. In fact, it's considered rude for a restaurant to rush customers by setting down coffee with dessert. Then finally, the third part, a spirit, like *grappa* or *amaro,* is served as a *digestivo,* an aid to digestion.

For me, one of the biggest differences between Italy and the United States is the restaurant experience. In Italy when I sit down to dinner in a restaurant, that table is mine for the night. I am never rushed.

The courses are served in a leisurely fashion—not only because the food in Italy is usually made to order, but because they want us to have time between courses to digest and to build anticipation and an appetite for the next course. My plate isn't removed until everyone else at the table has also finished eating.

I especially like the after-dessert *digestivo* tradition in Italy. My favorites are the homemade ones, brought out by the chef himself and poured with a flourish as a final culinary gift. I've had all kinds of delicious concoctions, and the chefs have shared their recipes generously.

meno siamo a tavola, e più si mangia.

THE LESS TIME WE SPEND AT THE TABLE, THE MORE WE EAT.

alchermes

MAKES ABOUT 1½ QUARTS (1.4 LITERS)

REGION: Tuscany and throughout Italy

This spicy-sweet liqueur with a lovely floral aroma and distinctive bright red color is a key ingredient in many, many classic Italian desserts, including *zuppa inglese*. Despite the fact that *alchermes* is listed as an ingredient in dozens and dozens of recipes in any Italian dessert cookbook, it isn't yet available in the States. Luckily it's simple to make, using ingredients you probably already have in your pantry. One splash adds lots of flavor—a sort of spiked spice-route brew.

chi vuota il bicchiere tutto in una volta, è un ubriacone; chi in due, è bene educato; chi in tre, appartiene ai superbi.

IF YOU EMPTY YOUR GLASS
IN ONE GULP YOU'RE A DRUNK;
IN TWO YOU'RE POLITE,
IN THREE, YOU'RE PRETENTIOUS.

Pure grain alcohol or vodka ✖ 2⅓ cups (18 ½ fluid ounces/555 milliliters)

Cinnamon ✖ 1 (2-inch/5-centimeter) stick

Ground coriander ✖ ½ teaspoon

Mace ✖ 1 to 2 blades; or ground mace ✖ ¼ teaspoon

Ground cardamom ✖ ¼ teaspoon

Cloves ✖ 4 whole

Candied orange peel ✖ 3 tablespoons

Star anise ✖ 3 whole

½ vanilla bean, cut into small pieces

Sugar ✖ 2½ cups (17½ ounces/500 grams)

Warm water ✖ 2 cups

Rose water ✖ 7 tablespoons (3½ fluid ounces/105 milliliters)

Red food coloring

Combine the alcohol and 1¼ cups (12 fluid ounces/360 milliliters) water in a sealable glass container such as a Mason jar. Add the cinnamon, coriander, mace, cardamom, cloves, candied orange peel, star anise, and vanilla and stir to combine. Leave the container, sealed, at room temperature for 2 weeks, shaking the container daily to combine the ingredients.

Combine the sugar and warm water and stir until the sugar dissolves. Add to the alcohol mixture and seal the container. Let it sit for another day or two, then taste, and add more sugar or water, if you like. Strain the liqueur into a clean sealable glass container and stir in the rose water and enough red food coloring to get a bright red color.

limoncello

MAKES ABOUT 1¼ QUARTS (1.2 LITERS)

REGION: Campania, especially the Amalfi coast

Keep it in the freezer and serve it icy cold. Limoncello is fabulous sipped with dessert but is also great splashed on fresh fruit salad or ice cream.

non domandare all'oste se ha buon vino.
DON'T BOTHER ASKING THE BARTENDER IF THE WINE IS GOOD.

Using a vegetable peeler, peel the yellow zest from the lemons, in long strips. Put the peels and alcohol in a 1½- to 2-quart (1.4- to 2-liter) sealable glass container, such as a Mason jar. Seal and set aside for 2 weeks in a cool, dark place.

Bring 3 cups (24 fluid ounces/720 milliliters) water to a boil in a saucepan and stir in the sugar. Simmer until the sugar is dissolved, then remove from the heat and let cool to room temperature. Stir the cooled sugar syrup into the alcohol mixture. Taste, and add more sugar, if you like. Seal, and store for another 2 weeks in a cool, dark place, then pour the mixture through a fine-mesh sieve, discarding the peels.

Store in the freezer. Serve icy cold.

Lemons ✖ 6

Pure grain alcohol or vodka ✖ 2 cups (16 fluid ounces/480 milliliters)

Sugar ✖ 2 cups (14 ounces/400 grams)

cream of limoncello

Crema di limoncello

MAKES ABOUT 1½ QUARTS (1.4 LITERS)

REGION: Campania, especially the Amalfi coast

A creamy version of limoncello. Much more delicious homemade than what's available commercially. It's like a grown-up lemon creamsicle!

Lemons ✘ 6

Pure grain alcohol or vodka ✘ 2 cups (16 fluid ounces/480 milliliters)

Unsweetened condensed skim milk ✘ 2 cups (16 fluid ounces/480 milliliters)

1 vanilla bean, cut into pieces

Sugar ✘ 2 cups (14 ounces/400 grams)

Heavy cream ✘ 1 cup (8 fluid ounces/ 240 milliliters)

Using a vegetable peeler, peel the yellow zest from the lemons, in long strips. Put the peels and alcohol in a 1½- to 2-quart (1.4- to 2-liter) sealable glass container, such as a Mason jar. Seal and set aside for 2 weeks in a cool, dark place.

Bring the condensed milk and vanilla to a low boil in a saucepan and stir in the sugar. Simmer until the sugar is dissolved, then remove from the heat and let cool to room temperature. Stir the cooled syrup and the cream into the alcohol mixture. Taste, and add more sugar if you like.

Seal and store for another 2 weeks in the refrigerator, then strain the mixture through a fine-mesh sieve, discarding the peels and vanilla bean.

Seal and store in the freezer or refrigerator. Shake gently before serving. Serve cold.

chocolate liqueur

Liquore al cioccolato

MAKES ABOUT 1 QUART (960 MILLILITERS)
REGION: Throughout Italy

Creamy chocolate liqueur with a touch of almond, it's like a candy bar in a glass.

Bring the milk to a boil in a saucepan over medium-high heat, add the sugar, and stir until the sugar is dissolved. Remove from the heat and stir in the cocoa powder until well combined. Let cool to room temperature, stir in the alcohol and Amaretto, and pour through a fine-mesh sieve or through cheesecloth. Pour into a sealable glass container, such as a Mason jar, and store in the freezer. Serve icy cold.

Milk ✖ 2 cups (16 fluid ounces/ 480 milliliters)

Sugar ✖ 2 cups (14 ounces/400 grams)

Unsweetened cocoa powder ✖ 4 tablespoons

Pure grain alcohol or vodka ✖ 1½ cups (12 fluid ounces/360 milliliters)

Amaretto or other almond liqueur ✖ ½ cup (4 fluid ounces/120 milliliters)

chocolate comes to italy

Christopher Columbus was the first European to ever set eyes on cacao beans, a New World food, and they first entered Europe through Spain. Turin was the first Italian city to receive cocoa beans, a gift of the royal court of Madrid in 1559. By the 1700s, Turin was an international chocolate capital, with the city's producers exporting 750 pounds (340 kilograms) a day to Austria, Switzerland, Germany, and France. According to Sandro Doglio's 1995 book *Il dizionario di gastronomia del Piemonte,* even Swiss chocolatiers came to Turin to learn their craft.

CHOCOLATE IN BARS

Most bars sell chocolates for consumption on-site, and many have a large brandy snifter full of *Baci*—Perugina's chocolate kisses—for sale. A customer buys one for his date or as a way to meet someone. How much more charmingly Italian to be offered a chocolate "kiss" than to be greeted with, "Can I buy you a drink?"

coffee liqueur

Liquore al caffè

MAKES ABOUT 1 QUART (960 MILLILITERS)

REGION: Throughout Italy

Milk ✱ 2 cups (16 fluid ounces/
480 milliliters)

Sugar ✱ 2 cups (14 ounces/400 grams)

1 vanilla bean

Instant espresso powder ✱ 3 to 4
tablespoons (¼ to ⅓ ounces/9 to 12 grams)

Pure grain alcohol or vodka ✱ 1½ cups
(12 fluid ounces/360 milliliters)

Amaretto or other almond liqueur ✱ ½ cup
(4 fluid ounces/120 milliliters)

Bring the milk to a boil in a saucepan over medium-high heat, add the sugar and vanilla bean, and stir until the sugar is dissolved. Remove from the heat and stir in the espresso powder until well combined. Let cool to room temperature, stir in the alcohol, and taste and add more sugar, if you like. Pour through a fine-mesh sieve or through cheesecloth, discarding the vanilla bean, and pour into a sealable glass container, such as a Mason jar, and store in the freezer. Serve icy cold.

mixed berry liqueur

Liquore di frutta di bosco

MAKES ABOUT 1 QUART (960 MILLILITERS)

REGION: Throughout Italy

Berries, such as raspberries, blackberries, or
blueberries ✱ 1 pound (455 grams)

Pure grain alcohol or vodka ✱ 2 cups (16
fluid ounces/480 milliliters)

Sugar ✱ 1 cup (7 ounces/200 grams)

Combine the berries and alcohol in a sealable glass container, such as a Mason jar, seal, and let rest in a cool, dark place for 45 days.

Press the mixture through a fine-mesh sieve, discarding any pulp. Bring 2 cups (16 fluid ounces/480 milliliters) water to a boil, then stir in the sugar until dissolved. Let cool to room temperature, then pour into the liquid, stirring until well combined. Pour into a clean sealable glass container and store in the freezer. Serve icy cold.

UN ALTRO MODO

Cream Berry Liqueur: Substitute 1 cup (8 fluid ounces/240 milliliters) milk and 1 cup (8 fluid ounces/240 milliliters) heavy cream for the 2 cups (16 fluid ounces/480 milliliters) water. Shake well before serving.

espresso glossary

ESPRESSO LUNGO: Italian espresso is generally made with 1½ fluid ounces/45 milliliters water. A milder version, made with an ounce or two more water, is called *espresso lungo. Caffè Americano,* with even more hot water added, is very weak.

ESPRESSO RISTRETTO: The opposite of *lungo.* With only 1 ounce/30 milliliters water, it is even more concentrated than normal espresso.

ESPRESSO DOPPIO: Two shots of espresso.

ESPRESSO MACCHIATO: A shot of espresso "marked" or "stained" with a tablespoon of frothy hot milk. The reverse, *latte macchiato,* is a tall glass of hot steamed milk "marked" with a shot of espresso.

ESPRESSO CORRETTO: Most often it's a shot of espresso "corrected" (or perhaps better translated as "improved") with a splash of grappa or, often enough, sambuca, brandy, or whiskey. In Italy espresso is not served with lemon peel.

That's a purely American invention that started back at the turn of the century when Italians arriving in the States couldn't find their beloved espresso so added a bit of lemon thinking it might improve the flavor of American coffee.

CAPPUCCINO: Also called, in some regions, *cappuccio,* a single shot of espresso topped with steamed and frothy milk and served in a 5- to 6-ounce/150- to 180-milliliter cup. In Italy, cappuccino is strictly a morning drink, never drunk after lunchtime. The name comes from the color of the robes of the Capuchin monks.

CAFFÈ HAG: Hag is a popular brand of decaf coffee in Italy, and it often simply designates a decaffeinated espresso, or *caffè decaffinato.*

CAFFÈ D'ORZO: Barley coffee, a caffeine-free coffee substitute that can be ordered in any of the above variations, including *cappuccino d'orzo.*

*il caffe deve essere caldo come l'inferno, nero come il diavolo,
puro come un angelo, e dolce come l'amore.*

COFFEE SHOULD BE HOT AS HELL, BLACK AS THE DEVIL,
PURE AS AN ANGEL, AND AS SWEET AS LOVE.

walnut liqueur

la guazza di san giovanni cura tutti i malanni.

SAN GIOVANNI MORNING DEW HEALS ILLS.

Nocino

MAKES ABOUT 1½ QUARTS (1.4 LITERS)

REGION: Northern Italy, especially Emilia-Romagna

Nocino is an aromatic *digestivo,* made from unripe walnuts traditionally gathered on the eve of the Feast of San Giovanni, June 24, on *La Notte delle Vergini Scalze,* or Evening of the Barefoot Virgins. If you don't have shoeless virgins willing to collect nuts for you, I'm sure your greengrocer can find some. It's certainly worth a little asking around to find unripe walnuts, which have a bright green rind and a fantastic fragrance, to make this delicious drink.

Green walnuts, with husks ✖ 20

Pure grain alcohol or vodka, grappa, or other neutral spirit ✖ 4 cups (32 fluid ounces/960 milliliters)

Cinnamon ✖ 1 (2-inch/5-centimeter) stick

Cloves ✖ 6 whole

Grated zest of 1 small lemon

White wine ✖ 1 cup (8 fluid ounces/240 milliliters)

Sugar ✖ 2 cups (14 ounces/400 grams)

Wash and dry the walnuts. Cut them into quarters (they will be soft, as the hard outer shell we normally associate with walnuts hasn't formed yet).

Put the walnuts, alcohol, cinnamon, cloves, lemon zest, and wine in a large sealable container and stir well. Seal tightly and place in a sunny spot for at least 40 days, and preferably 3 months, shaking it once daily to recombine all the ingredients.

Bring the sugar and 1 cup (8 fluid ounces/240 milliliters) bottled or filtered water to a boil. Let cool to room temperature. Strain the walnut liquid through a paper filter or fine-mesh sieve and stir in the sugar syrup. Taste and add more sugar or water, if you like. Put into a clean sealable container and allow to rest for at least 2 months. It only improves with age.

UN ALTRO MODO

Nocino al caffè: Add 10 to 12 espresso coffee beans with the other spices.

Nocino dei frati: Add 3 mace blades, several slices of nutmeg, and 1 vanilla bean, in addition to the other spices.

anything-goes grappa

Grappa aromatizzata

MAKES ABOUT 1 QUART (960 MILLILITERS)

REGION: Throughout Italy, especially northern Italy

I love trying all the amazing after-dinner *digestivi* my Italian friends make. I've had grappa infused with just about every herb, spice, and fruit imaginable. They're all good, and the Italian secret to really incredible infused spirits is not to mix too many flavors together. Besides the grappa, aim for no more than three ingredients. Some of my favorite combinations are: fig and honey; celery and lemon; pear and basil; fresh laurel and lemon verbena; and rosemary, apple, and chamomile. You can strain the ingredients after a month or two, or leave them in. I prefer them left in and served in a decorative decanter.

Combine the grappa, sugar, and infusion ingredients in a sealable container. Allow to infuse for at least 1 month before serving. Add more sugar to taste, if you like.

Grappa ✕ 1 bottle (25 fluid ounces/ 750 milliliters)

Sugar or honey ✕ ½ cup (3½ ounces/ 100 grams)

Infusion ingedients such as fruit, herbs, and spices

glossary of italian dessert wines and liqueurs

ALCHERMES (PAGE 182): *Alchermes,* a spicy-sweet bright red liqueur, has been popular in Italy since the Renaissance. Pope Clemente VII considered it healthful, going so far as to call it "the elixir of long life." *Alchermes* was supposedly brought by Maria de' Medici to France, where it was called *liquore de' Medici.* Originally the shell of the cochineal bug was used to color the liqueur, but today it's made with artificial colorings.

ALEATICO DELL'ELBA PASSITO: An exceptional dessert wine with lovely aroma of roses and dark berries awarded the special *Denominazione d'Origine Controllata e Garantita* (DOCG) designation.

AMARETTO: Amaretto, "little bitter," is a sweet almond-flavored liqueur cordial. Amaretto is an ingredient in hundreds of dessert recipes and is also paired with all sorts of Italian sweets, especially crunchy *amaretti* cookies. One of Italy's bestselling brands of amaretto is Di Saronno Originale.

AMARO: *Amaro* is the term for a general category of bittersweet digestives, after-dinner drinks thought to aid digestion. *Amaro,* which means "bitter," is generally made from various spices, herbs, fruits, and alcohol. Popular since the Middle Ages, monks originally created these drinks as medicinal remedies. There are hundreds, if not thousands, of different types of *amaro* in Italy, with each region, city, and even village claiming its own local specialty.

ASTI MOSCATO: A dessert wine made in the Asti region of Piedmont using *moscato* grapes. It's less bubbly than Asti Spumante.

ASTI SPUMANTE: Asti Spumante, a sparkling dessert wine, is made with the *moscato bianco* grapes from the Langhe, Monferrato, and Roero areas of Piedmont. Asti Spumante is a DOCG wine, meaning it is officially certified and guaranteed as to process and origin. Asti, an easy-to-drink wine, has a moderate alcohol content of 7 to 9.5 percent. In Italy, it is served in bowl-shaped glasses, rather than the thinner Champagne flutes. The thinking is that the narrow flute exaggerates Asti's sweetness, concentrating the liquid on the tip of the tongue, where the sweet taste buds are situated.

BAROLO CHINATO: An after-dinner *digestivo* from the Piedmont region, made with Barolo wine that has been steeped with different spices and herbs, such as cinnamon, coriander, mint, and vanilla. It is a very smooth, aromatic beverage that pairs beautifully with chocolate.

BRACHETTO D'ACQUI: A red sparkling dessert wine produced in the Piedmont. It is a blend of *aleatico* and *moscato nero* grapes.

FRANGELICO: A hazelnut liqueur in a trademarked bottle shaped like a monk. Great for both drinking and as a dessert ingredient.

GALLIANO: A bright yellow liqueur, Galliano is a mix of dozens of herbs and spices. First made in Livorno in 1896 and named for the nineteenth-century Italian war hero Giuseppe Galliano. Used in cocktails and as an after-dinner *digestivo,* it's also a terrific flavoring for various dessert recipes.

GRAPPA: Grappa is a fragrant spirit, 75 to 120 proof, made from the grape skins and other solids left over from the winemaking process. The name *grappa* most likely comes from the Italian for "bunch of grapes," *grappolo d'uva.* In Italy, grappa is enjoyed after dessert, served in small, tulip-shaped or short grappa glasses. It is also exceptional paired with Italian chocolates. A splash of grappa is often added to espresso to create *caffè corretto.*

LIMONCELLO (PAGE 183): A lemon liqueur from the Amalfi coast, Calabria, and Sicily. Made by steeping lemon peels in alcohol and sugar, it can be drunk at room temperature or icy cold. Wonderful with Italian cookies, pastries, and cakes, limoncello is also an ingredient in many desserts.

MALVASIA DELLE LIPARI: An amber-colored DOC dessert wine from Sicily with an apricot-honey taste and a lovely aroma.

MARASCHINO LIQUEUR: A clear cherry liqueur made from northern Italian *marasca* cherries (not the same as maraschino cherries found in supermarkets). Used in many traditional Italian desserts.

MARSALA: Marsala is a DOC golden-colored fortified wine made with grapes grown in the Marsala region of Sicily. Marsala is made both sweet and dry. The dry is enjoyed chilled as an aperitif, while the sweet is sipped at room temperature as a dessert wine. Marsala is used extensively in Italian cooking, especially in making sweets such as the classic *zabaglione.*

MOSCADELLO DI MONTALCINO: A DOC dessert wine from the Montalcino region of Tuscany made with aromatic white muscat grapes. It is produced in three versions: still, sparkling, and late-harvest.

NOCINO (PAGE 188): *Nocino* is a dark-colored *digestivo* made from unripe green walnuts.

PASSITO: *Passito* is a dessert wine made by pressing partially dried grapes, dried to concentrate their sugar and flavor.

PASSITO DI PANTELLERIA: One of Italy's most acclaimed *passito* wines. In 1971, this fine dessert wine from Sicily became only the third Italian wine to receive DOC status. It has a lovely bouquet and a velvety sweet yet crisp flavor.

SAMBUCA: A colorless *digestivo* liqueur flavored with star anise. Sambuca is splashed in coffee, or served neat, sometimes served *con la mosca* ("with flies"), topped with three toasted espresso beans. Besides giving a little caffeine kick, chewing on the beans highlights sambuca's flavor.

SASSOLINO: A liqueur from the town of Sassolino in Modena. Flavored with star anise, it's an ingredient in many Emilia desserts.

STREGA LIQUEUR: *Strega,* "witch," is a yellow liqueur made from more than seventy ingredients, including saffron, which gives it its color. Used as a *digestivo* and in dessert recipes.

VIN SANTO: *Vin santo,* "holy wine," is a smooth amber-colored wine made from Malvasia and Trebbiano grapes. Although made in many parts of Italy, it is most often associated with Tuscany, where it is often paired with *cantucci,* the area's crunchy almond biscotti.

italian alps spiked coffee

Caffè alla valdostana

SERVES 4

REGION: Valle d'Aosta

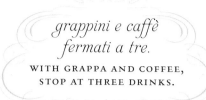

This aromatic coffee—seasoned with sugar, grappa, and citrus zest—is a favorite northern Italian après-ski treat. It's served in a communal drinking vessel called *grolla* or *coppa dell'amicizia*, "friendship cup," a handsome carved shallow bowl with 6 to 8 drinking spouts. The idea is to sip at one spout, and then pass the cup clockwise to the next person, who sips from the next spout. Sharing a *grolla* with friends is a must for anyone visiting the Valle d'Aosta region of Italy. If you have a *grolla*, sprinkle the inner rim and each spout with sugar, pour in all the ingredients, and ignite the coffee, allowing it to burn until the sugar caramelizes.

Here's an alternate recipe in case you don't have a proper *grolla*.

Sugar

Grappa or genepy (see Note) ✖ ½ cup
(4 fluid ounces/120 milliliters)

1 orange

Freshly brewed hot espresso ✖ 4 long shots
(about 12 fluid ounces/360 milliliters—about 1½ cups)

Ground cinnamon or ground nutmeg

Put some sugar in a shallow dish. Moisten the rims of 4 mugs with grappa and dip each into the sugar. Put a teaspoon or two of sugar into each mug.

Cut 4 long strips of zest from the orange, using a vegetable peeler. Divide among the 4 mugs.

Pour a shot of espresso into each mug and add a pinch of cinnamon or nutmeg and 1 ounce (30 milliliters) of the grappa to each mug.

NOTE: *Genepy*, also called "*génépi*," made with flowers and herbs from the area, is a *digestivo* popular in the French and Italian Alps, especially in the Val d'Aosta region.

espresso sweet tweets

- CAMARETTO: Espresso with caramel and a shot of Amaretto di Saronno, topped with whipped cream and crushed *amaretti* cookies.

- CIOCAFFÈ: Espresso with chocolate syrup, topped with whipped cream and grated chocolate.

- BOSCO: Espresso with pastry cream, topped with whipped cream and fresh berries.

- BABY CAFFÈ: Espresso with warm milk, Nutella, and whipped cream. Served with a cookie.

caffè shakerato

SERVES 2
REGION: Throughout Italy

Freshly brewed espresso and a bit of sugar syrup shaken with ice in a cocktail shaker.
The result is a lovely frothy top on a sweet refreshing drink. It's a delightful break from the same-old, same-old iced coffee and very popular during Italy's hot summers. If you'd like to get fancy, serve this drink in chilled martini glasses.

tazza e cucchiaio.
CUP AND SPOON. (SAID OF TWO PEOPLE WHO ARE ALWAYS TOGETHER.)

Sugar ✖ ¼ cup (1¾ ounces/50 grams)

Freshly brewed hot espresso or coffee ✖
2 long shots (about 6 fluid ounces/
180 milliliters)

Bring ¼ cup (2 fluid ounces/60 milliliters) water to a boil in a small saucepan. Add the sugar, stir until dissolved, and simmer for a few minutes to thicken. Let cool to room temperature, then store in a sealed container in the refrigerator until ready to use. The syrup stays fresh for a month or longer.

Put 8 to 10 ice cubes in a chilled cocktail shaker, add sugar syrup to taste, and hot espresso or coffee and shake vigorously for at least 10 seconds. Divide the mixture between 2 chilled glasses. Open the shaker and, using a spoon, remove the coffee foam, placing a little on top of each glass. Serve immediately.

italian hot chocolate

SERVES 3 TO 4
REGION: Throughout Italy

Dense and fudgy.

Milk ✖ 2 cups (16 fluid ounces/
480 milliliters)

Sugar ✖ ⅓ cup (2¼ ounces/65 grams), plus more to taste

Cornstarch or potato starch ✖ 1 tablespoon

Unsweetened cocoa powder ✖
2 to 3 tablespoons

Ground cinnamon, optional

In a small saucepan, combine the milk, sugar, cornstarch, and cocoa powder and whisk until smooth and well combined. Heat over medium-high heat and bring to a low boil, whisking constantly, until the mixture thickens, about 2 minutes. Serve immediately, topped with a sprinkle of cinnamon, if you like.

CHAPTER TEN

basics

pastry cream

Crema pasticcera

MAKES 6 CUPS (1½ QUARTS/1.4 LITERS)

nun te piglià collera ca 'o zucchero va caro.

DON'T GET UPSET THAT SUGAR IS EXPENSIVE. (NEAPOLITAN EXPRESSION MEANING IT ISN'T WORTH THE WORRY.)

Creamy custard seasoned with aromatic vanilla, this is an absolute basic, used to make hundreds of classic Italian desserts, including *torta della nonna* and *zuppa inglese.*

It's also served plain, accompanied by fresh fruit, slices of *pandoro* or *panettone,* or cookies. This is a simple and very forgiving recipe.

Egg yolks ✕ 8 large

Sugar ✕ ½ cup (3½ ounces/100 grams)

All-purpose flour ✕ ½ cup (2 ounces/55 grams)

Milk ✕ 3 cups (24 fluid ounces/720 milliliters)

Heavy cream ✕ 1 cup (8 fluid ounces/240 milliliters)

Pure vanilla extract ✕ 1 tablespoon

In a bowl, combine the egg yolks and sugar and beat with an electric mixer or whisk until creamy and light yellow. Mix in the flour, 1 tablespoon at a time, until smooth.

Put the milk, cream, and vanilla in a saucepan and heat over low heat until bubbles begin to appear around the edge of the pan. Do not boil. Gradually beat in the egg yolk mixture, making sure to beat until there are no lumps. Return to low heat and cook, stirring constantly with a wooden spoon, until the pastry cream thickens, about 3 minutes. Do not overcook. The mixture should be thick, but not stiff. It will solidify as it cools.

Immediately remove from the heat and pour into a bowl. Cover with plastic wrap, with the wrap touching the surface of the pastry cream so it doesn't form a skin. Refrigerate until cold, at least 4 hours.

UN ALTRO MODO

Crema pasticcera al caffè: Add 1½ tablespoons instant espresso powder.

Crema pasticcera al cioccolato: Add 3 ounces/85 grams grated dark chocolate and 1 tablespoon unsweetened cocoa powder.

Crema pasticcera al limone: Omit the vanilla and add the grated zest and juice of 1 lemon.

pie crust dough

Pasta frolla

MAKES ENOUGH DOUGH FOR 1 DOUBLE-CRUST PIE,
OR 2 SINGLE-CRUST PIES

This is the mainstay Italian crust. Similar to short-crust pastry, it's a very forgiving dough, virtually impossible to mess up. Even if it breaks apart a little as you're putting it into the pie pan, all you have to do is press it together with your fingers. Roll it out on a sheet of lightly floured parchment paper, as the dough is very sticky.

All-purpose flour ✖ 1⅞ cups
(8½ ounces/240 grams)

Sugar ✖ ¾ cup (5¼ ounces/150 grams)

Butter ✖ 8 tablespoons (4 ounces/
115 grams), softened, cut into pieces

Eggs ✖ 2 large

Egg yolks ✖ 2 large

Grated zest of 1 lemon

Salt ✖ ¼ teaspoon

Liqueur, such as Maraschino or Sassolino ✖
2 tablespoons, optional

In a large bowl or on a work surface, mix together the flour, sugar, and butter pieces with a wooden spoon until the mixture resembles coarse sand. Form a well in the center and add the eggs, egg yolks, lemon zest, salt, and liqueur (if using). Gradually stir in the flour mixture, until thoroughly combined. Shape the dough into a ball, wrap in a sheet of plastic wrap, and refrigerate for at least 1 hour before rolling out.

italian sponge cake

Pan di spagna

MAKES ENOUGH FOR TWO 9-INCH/23-CENTIMETER ROUND THIN CAKE
LAYERS, OR ONE 9-INCH/23-CENTIMETER ROUND THICK CAKE LAYER

Pan di spagna, "bread of Spain," is a key ingredient in hundreds of classic Italian desserts like *zuccoto* and Sicilian cassata. *Pan di spagna*'s light and airy texture absorbs fillings amazingly well, so it stacks wonderfully, allowing you to create tall, moist layer cakes.

Preheat the oven to 350°F (180°C). Lightly butter and flour one or two 9- or 10-inch (23- to 25-centimeter) springform cake pans.

Combine the whole eggs and sugar in a stand mixer and beat on high speed for 15 minutes, until the mixture quadruples in volume.

Add the egg yolks and beat on high speed for 5 minutes. The mixture should be thick enough to write with. Sift the flour and potato starch gradually into the egg-sugar mixture, incorporating a little at a time, mixing each inclusion of flour delicately with a spatula, scooping from the bottom up, so you do not deflate the eggs. Mix in the vanilla and lemon zest until just blended, then divide the batter between the prepared pans.

Bake for about 30 minutes, until light golden and a toothpick inserted in the center of the cake comes out clean. Do not overbake. It will dry and set as it cools.

Turn out onto a wire rack and let cool to room temperature.

Butter and flour for the pan

Eggs ✖ 4 large

Sugar ✖ 1 cup (8 ounces/225 grams)
plus 2 tablespoons

Egg yolks ✖ 8 large

00 flour ✖ 1⅞ cups (7 ounces/200 grams)

Potato starch or cornstarch ✖ ¼ cup
(1 ounce/30 grams)

Pure vanilla extract ✖ 2 teaspoons

Grated zest of ½ lemon

egg pasta

MAKES 1 POUND (455 GRAMS)

buon vino, tavola lunga.
GOOD WINE KEEPS
US AT THE DINNER LONGER.

This straightforward recipe is perfect for making *torta riccolina* (page 153) and is also great with savory sauces.

Semolina or all-purpose flour ✖ 1¾ cups (10 ounces/280 grams)

Eggs ✖ 3 large

Egg yolk ✖ 1 large

Mound the flour in a large bowl. Make a deep well in the center of the mound and add the eggs and egg yolk. Beat the eggs with a fork, then gradually incorporate a little flour at a time. Knead the dough for about 10 minutes, until it feels silky. Working in sections, roll it out with a rolling pin or pass it through a pasta machine, following the manufacturer's instructions. Cut the pasta into thin strips and toss lightly with semolina flour to keep it from sticking.

lemon jam

Marmellata di limoni

MAKES AS MUCH AS YOU LIKE

I got this recipe from an adorable grandma in Basilicata, Franca Artuso, whose pantry of home-canned foods was better stocked than most supermarkets. She kept pulling out one jar after another—home-cured olives, peaches in brandy, sun-dried tomato paste, and dozens of different jams. If it fell off a tree, she made jam out of it. This is one of my favorites. I especially like that you use the entire lemon, so nothing is wasted. It's good on bread, with cheeses, or as pie filling.

Small seedless lemons

Sugar

Pierce the lemons all over with a fork. Put the lemons in a large bowl of water for 3 days, replacing the water twice each day.

Cut the lemons, skin and pulp, into very tiny pieces either with a knife by hand or, preferably, in a food processor. Weigh the resulting lemon mass and measure out that weight in sugar. Combine the lemons and sugar in a saucepan and cook over medium-low heat until thickened, about 40 minutes, stirring frequently with a wooden spoon. Put into sterilized jars or keep refrigerated.

quick candied orange peel

Scorzette di arance candite, metodo veloce

MAKES 1½ CUPS (12 FLUID OUNCES/360 MILLILITERS)

*chini toccada sumeli
si lingidi su idu.*

WHO TOUCHES HONEY WILL
SURELY LICK HIS FINGER.

To make candied orange peel you usually have to carefully cut off the skin and remove the white pith, but in this Italian method you actually leave it on and even some of the orange itself. This cuts prep time way down, makes for a softer candied peel, and actually adds to the flavor.

In Italy, candied orange peels are often served after dessert as a little nibble to keep you lingering at the table. They are terrific plain or dipped in dark chocolate. Chop and add them to cookie or cake recipes or even to rice pudding, custard, sorbet, or gelato.

Cut the oranges into quarters, then slice each quarter into slices about ⅓ inch (8 millimeters) thick. Bring a large pot of water to a boil, then add the orange slices. Bring the water back to a boil, then drain. Repeat once more to remove any of the orange peels' remaining bitterness.

Combine the orange slices and sugar with 4 cups (1 quart/ 960 milliliters) water and bring to a boil. Lower the heat to very low and simmer until all the water evaporates, about 2 hours. Let cool in the pan, then spread the orange slices on a baking sheet or wire rack, sprinkle with a little sugar, and air dry for 24 hours. The peels can be stored in the refrigerator in an airtight container for several months.

Navel oranges ✽ 6 large

Sugar ✽ 2¼ cups (15¾ ounces/450 grams), plus more for drying

cherry jam

Marmellata di ciliegie

MAKES 1¼ CUPS (12 FLUID OUNCES/360 MILLILITERS)

In Italy, fresh cherries are often served in a large bowl of water and ice. This recipe, made without pectin or a fuss, captures their summer flavor. Sweet and simple.

Combine the cherries and sugar in a saucepan, cover with plastic wrap, and let macerate at room temperature overnight or for 12 hours. Put the pan over low heat and simmer for about 45 minutes, until thickened. Let cool to room temperature, then either leave it chunky or puree the mixture in a mini food processor. Stir in the lemon zest. Store in an airtight container in the refrigerator. Stays fresh for 6 weeks or more.

Pitted cherries ✽ 1 pound/455 grams

Sugar ✽ 1¼ cups (8¾ ounces/250 grams)

Grated zest of ½ lemon

grape jam

Marmellata d'uva

MAKES 3 CUPS (24 FLUID OUNCES/720 MILLILITERS)

Dark, densely flavorful, and aromatic, this classic Italian grape preserve is made without sugar and you don't even need to add pectin, as the apple provides enough naturally.

chi mangia l'uva per capodanno maneggia i quattrini tutto l'anno.

WHO EVER EATS GRAPES ON NEW YEAR WILL HAVE GOOD LUCK ALL YEAR.

Black grapes ✖ 4 pounds (1.8 kilograms), stemmed and seeded

Apple ✖ 1 cored, peeled, and diced

Combine the grapes and apple in a large saucepan and cook over very low heat for 4 to 5 hours, stirring occasionally. Or you can put them in the oven at 200°F (95°C) for 6 to 8 hours, until very, very thick. Let cool to room temperature, put in a clean jar, and refrigerate. Stays fresh for 6 weeks or more.

peach almond marmalade

Marmellata di pesche all'amaretto

MAKES ABOUT 3 CUPS (24 FLUID OUNCES/720 MILLILITERS)

Peaches with a double hint of almond.

Yellow peaches ✖ 1 pound/455 grams

White peaches ✖ 1 pound/455 grams

Sugar ✖ 2 cups (14 ounces/400 grams)

Almond liqueur, such as Amaretto ✖ 5 tablespoons (2½ fluid ounces/75 milliliters)

5 whole blanched almonds, lightly toasted and finely crushed

Pit and coarsely chop the peaches, leaving the skins on. Combine them in a bowl with the sugar and refrigerate for at least 12 hours or overnight.

Put the resulting juice in a wide saucepan and bring to a boil. Lower the heat and simmer until the liquid reduces by half, then add the fruit pieces. Simmer the fruit over very low heat for about 1½ hours, until the mixture thickens. (Don't worry if it seems too liquidy; it will condense as it cools. If you'd like to test the jam, put a tiny plate in the freezer for 1 hour. Place a few drops of the jam onto the icy cold plate and tilt the plate. If the jam runs down slowly, it's ready.)

When thick, add the liqueur and almonds and continue to simmer for another 5 minutes so the alcohol evaporates. Pour into sterilized Mason jars, or if you're refrigerating the jam, into clean containers.

italian sweets makers

BAULI
Via Verdi, 31, 37060
Castel D'Azzano, Veneto
www.bauliusa.com

CORSINI BISCOTTI
Via Cellane, 9
Castel del Piano, Tuscany
www.corsinibiscotti.com

FALANGA/SABRA
Via Cosmo Mollica Alagona, 65
Catania, Sicily
www.falanga.eu

PERUGINA
Via Pievaiola, 06143
Perugia, Umbria
www.perugina.it

VENCHI
Via Cuneo, 45
12040 Castelletto
Cuneo, Piedmont
www.venchi.it

ASSOCIATION OF ITALIAN DESSERT AND PASTA MANUFACTURERS
AIDEPI (Associazione della Industrie del Dolce e della Pasta Italiane)
Via Rhodesia, 2
Rome
www.dolceitalia.com
www.dolceitalia.net
www.sweet-italy.com

online sources for ingredients

AMAZON
www.amazon.com

General source for all sorts of Italian products.

CHEF SHOP
www.chefshop.com

Offers a wide range of Italian sweets, including Venchi and Slitti chocolates, Falanga cookies, and Antica Torroneria Piedmontese *torrone*.

CHOCOSPHERE
www.chocosphere.com

For quality Italian chocolates.

DI ITALIA
www.ditalia.com

Pretty site with terrific assortment of extracts, including *millefiore* for making *pastiera*, plus cookies, cakes, chocolates, and more.

DOLCE ITALIA
www.dolceitalia.com

An information, not sales, site on a wide range of authentic Italian products, including cookies, holiday cakes, and chocolates.

GUSTOBENE
www.gustobene.com

Great source for a variety of Italian products, including cookies such as *amaretti*, *cantucci*, and *savoiardi*; espresso; jams, marmalades, and preserves; and honey, such as hard-to-find ones like *corbezzolo* honey from Sardinia.

IGOURMET
www.igourmet.com

General source for all sorts of Italian products, including jams, honeys, and nuts. Plus Corsini's *amaretti* and *cantucci* cookies, as well as Italian chocolates and candy, including *torrone*.

KING ARTHUR FLOUR
www.kingarthurflour.com

An excellent source for high-quality flours and all manner of baking products, King Arthur Italian-Style Flour is this Vermont-based company's version of 00 flour.

LICORICE INTERNATIONAL

www.licoriceinternational.com

For quality Italian licorice such as Liquirizia Amarelli, a Calabria-based maker since the 1700s.

PENZEYS SPICES

www.penzeys.com

For quality extracts, including almond, lemon, and vanilla, as well as whole vanilla beans and cinnamon sticks.

PERUGINA

www.perugina.com

For both Perugina chocolates and holiday cakes.

WORLD WIDE CHOCOLATE

www.worldwidechocolate.com

For quality Italian chocolate, chocolate candies, and cocoa powder.

ZINGERMAN'S

www.zingermans.com

Good source for hazelnut-chocolate spread, interesting Italian jams, including unusual licorice jam, 00 flour, and Paneangeli-brand baking products, such as vanilla-flavored confectioners' sugar and baking powder and baking soda packets are available in specialty gourmet markets and online on Amazon.com.

acknowledgments

These acknowledgements are long—much longer than for my other cookbooks. That's because this book is a collaboration between me and several hundred Italians! I made many, many friends along the way and here express my profound gratitude. If I have left any out, I beg them to accept my apologies.

Special thanks to the wonderful ITALIAN COMPANIES: Bauli, Corsini, Falanga-Sabra, Perugina, and Venchi, who arranged factory visits, answered my endless questions, provided recipes and technical advice, and graciously donated ingredients for recipe testing.

My gratitude to:

THE CHEFS: Fabio Picchi of Cibreo and Teatro del Sale in Florence for all his help on everything and anything Tuscan; award-winning pastry chef and distinguished member of the Accademia dei Maestri Pasticceri, Salvatore de Riso; Manuela and Carla Chicchi and Giuseppina of Hotel Pinamar; Giovanni Marzano of Grand Hotel Vesuvio; Vittorio and Guglielmo Mazzaro of Mazzaro Pasticceria, for teaching me all about *pastiera* and the wonders of Neapolitan espresso; Marco Vacchieri, Turin pastry chef; Giorgio and Antonio Giocio of 12 Apostoli in Verona; Michele Organte of RiescoinCucina; Daniele Fanti of Caffè Moakrico; Maria Grazia Carpentieri of La Tana del Lupo Agriturismo; Pier-paolo Ruta of Antica Dolceria Bonajuto for teaching me to make *mustazzoli* and *'mpanatigghi*; Corrado Assenza of Caffè Sicilia; Fabrizio Sepe of Le Tre Zucche Ristorante in Rome; and Domenico di Raffaele of the wonderful Hotel Caruso, a dynamo, who spent hours teaching me both in Italy and at my home in New York City.

ITALIAN COOKING SCHOOLS: Giovanna Muciaccia, of Insieme in Cucina in Puglia; Massimiliano Guidubaldi and Chiara Bertinelli of the Perugina Chocolate School; Olimpia Apogeo of Casa Artusia cooking school in Emilia-Romagna; Giorgia Chiatto of CucinAmica in Naples; Valeria Vocaturo of Cuoche Percaso in Rome; Franco Piumatti of Apro S. Cassiano; Rosita Di Antonio of Teramo; Erika Maggiora of Turino's Scuola la Maggiorana; Gabriella Mari of Scuola d'Arte Culinaria Cordon Bleu in Florence.

ITALIAN BLOGGERS: Thanks go to Agostina Battaglia (mypaneburroemarmellata.com) for the delicious and beautiful apple cake and fig focaccia; Sabrine d'Aubergine (fragoleamerenda.blogspot.com); Daniela Dal Ben (daniela diocleziano.blogspot.com); Daniela Delogu (SenzaPanna .blogspot.com); Rossella Di Bidino (machetiseimangiato .wordpress.com); Alessia Gavioli (muffinscookiesealtripas ticci.blogspot.com); Marina Malvezzi (mangiarebene.com);

Ornella Mirelli (ammodomio.blogspot.com) for the fabulous lemon granita that needs no scraping; Laura Monticelli (tavolefornelli.com); Pinella Orgiana (iDolcidiPinella.blogspot.com) for being my go-to person on zillions of minor—and some major—topics. Paola Sersante (aniceecannella.blogspot.com); Giulia Scarpaleggia (it.julskitchen.com); Giovanni Stecca (lavetrinadelnanni.blogspot.com); Sandra of Florence (gallina vecchiafabuonbrodo.blogspot.com); and Corrado Tumminelli (corradot.blogspot.com)

Italian foodie websites: Cooker.net and Barbara Gotti; Giallo Zafferano and Sonia Peronaci; Coquinaria.it; and most especially to Sandra Salerno of *Un Tocco di Zenzero* for connecting me with so many devoted Italian home bakers.

Gifted Italian home cooks: Franca Artuso, for patiently teaching me to make *panzarotti*, *carteddate*, and several jams; Alice De Ferrari; Isabella Morra; Giorgina Tobino for her wonderful *monte bianco*; and Roberto Gracci. Tiziana Ragusi and her son Roberto, mother-in-law Margherita Palumbi, and friends Rita Sampienri and Lea Lanciaprima.

Warmest appreciation to Oretta Zannini de Vita, noted Italian food historian and James Beard Award–winning author, for generously sharing her expertise, and Academia Barilla and Giancarlo Gonizzi, curator of their excellent culinary collection, for advice and assistance with historic cookbooks. My heart-felt appreciation to Gigi and Clara Padovani, noted Italian chocolate experts.

Thanks to the following for recipes and assistance: Ornella Franco and the Consorzio dell'Asti DOCG; Barbara Candolfini and the Emilia Romagna Region Tourist Board (www.travelemiliaromagna.com); Giorgia Zabbini and the Bologna Tourism Board; Carlo Odello and the Istituto Nazionale Espresso Italiano; Walter Santi of Ricette-Umbre and the Umbria Tourism Board.

Special thanks to: Luigi Falanga for being a wonderful host and guide in Sicily; Ubaldo and Corrado Corsini for an unforgettable Thanksgiving spent in Italy learning to make *cantucci*; G.B. Martelli of Venchi chocolates for recipes, cooking tips and mouth-watering chocolates; Janet d'Alesio and the staff at Hotel Caruso, who epitomize Italian hospitality; Marco Ribecchini; Ezio Falcone; Manlio Agliozzo; Alessandro and Cristiana Romano; Melika Swaczy; Linda Lappin, Mariuccia Chiantaretto Marolo; Mitì Vigliero, Fabrizia Lanza, Stefania Baggio, Rosangela Romano, Dorothea Traversa for her enthusiasm over her grandmother's *monte bianco*; Marta Bochicchio, Marco Ribecchini; and Chiara Zanini de Vita.

Deepest thanks to AIDEPI, *Associazione delle Industrie del Dolce e della Pasta Italiane*, for sharing their expertise on Italy's sweets traditions, introducing me to dozens of Italy's top dessert makers, and entrusting me with the joyful task of being their American ambassador. It's been a delight working with Mario Piccialuti, Patrizia De Vito, and all the exceptional AIDEPI member companies.

My appreciation to my recipe testers here in the States: Katie Adams, Jen Bernstein, Michael Farruggia, Sarah Kaufman, Susan Miccio and Iris Sroka. Special thanks to Moriah Simmons, a gifted pastry chef, and Janet Krupit, talented chocolatier, for their meticulous recipe testing. Thanks to Nach Waxman and Matt Sartwell of Kitchen Arts and Letters Bookstore and to all the great people at the Institute of Culinary Education for taste testing.

I am indebted to my gracious Italian friends Angela and Gianluca Traversa for everything from hosting me into their homes to arranging baking sessions with relatives and friends.

Heartfelt appreciation to Sarah Scaparone, journalist from Turin, for spending countless hours Skyping, answering questions, tracking down recipes, finding foodie websites, introducing me to chefs, shipping me books, making lists and checking them twice. I couldn't have written this book without her invaluable input!

Gratitude and love to my husband, Marc Segan, and our daughter, Samantha, for help with editing. After so much time spent in Italy speaking Italian my English prose was left with a thick Italian accent!

Special appreciation to Ellen Silverman, and to her team, for all the lovely photos. And finally, my deepest thanks to Leslie Stoker, publisher extraordinaire, Michelle Ishay-Cohen, art director, my editor, Marisa Bulzone, and the entire Stewart, Tabori & Chang family.

index